# Falaise 1944

## Death of an army

Campaign • 149

# Falaise 1944

## Death of an army

Ken Ford · Illustrated by Howard Gerrard

*Series editor* Lee Johnson

First published in Great Britain in 2005 by Osprey Publishing,
Midland House West Way, Botley, Oxford OX2 0PH, UK.
44-02 23rd St, Suite 219, Long Island City, NY 11101, USA
Email: info@ospreypublishing.com

A CIP catalogue record for this book is available from the British Library

ISBN 978 1 84176 626 3

Editor: Lee Johnson
Design: The Black Spot
Index by Glyn Sutcliffe
Maps by The Map Studio
3D bird's-eye views by The Black Spot
Battlescene artwork by Howard Gerrard
Originated by The Electronic Page Company, Cwmbran, UK
Printed in China through World Print Ltd.
Typeset in Helvetica Neue and ITC New Baskerville

09 10 11 12 13   16 15 14 13 12 11 10 9 8 7

FOR A CATALOGUE OF ALL BOOKS PUBLISHED BY OSPREY MILITARY
AND AVIATION PLEASE CONTACT:

Osprey Direct, c/o Random House Distribution Center,
400 Hahn Road, Westminster, MD 21157
Email: uscustomerservice@ospreypublishing.com

Osprey Direct, The Book Service Ltd, Distribution Centre,
Colchester Road, Frating Green, Colchester, Essex, CO7 7DW
E-mail: customerservice@ospreypublishing.com

**www.ospreypublishing.com**

## Artist's note

Readers may care to note that the original paintings from
which the colour plates in this book were prepared are
available for private sale. All reproduction copyright
whatsoever is retained by the Publishers. All enquiries
should be addressed to:

Howard Gerrard
11 Oaks Road
Tenterden
Kent
TN30 6RD
UK

The Publishers regret that they can enter into no
correspondence upon this matter.

## KEY TO MILITARY SYMBOLS

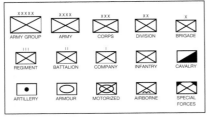

# CONTENTS

### ORIGINS OF THE BATTLE    7

### CHRONOLOGY    10

### OPPOSING COMMANDERS    13
Allied commanders • German commanders

### OPPOSING FORCES    18
German forces • Order of battle: German forces in Normandy and north-west France, July–August 1944

Allied forces • Order of battle: Allied forces, Normandy, July–August 1944

### OPPOSING PLANS    26
Allied plans • German plans

### THE FALAISE CAMPAIGN    30
The Breakout battles • The net begins to close

The encirclement • Operation *Tractable* • Destruction of an army

### AFTERMATH    87

### THE BATTLEFIELD TODAY    92

### BIBLIOGRAPHY    94

### INDEX    95

# ALLIED FRONTLINE BEFORE THE BREAKOUT BATTLES

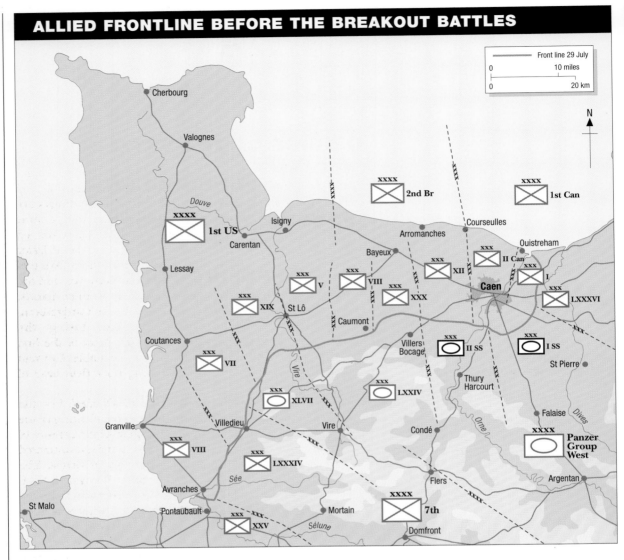

Front line 29 July

0 — 10 miles
0 — 20 km

N

Cherbourg

Valognes

*Douve*

Isigny

1st US

Carentan

Lessay

Coutances

St Lô

XIX

V

VIII

Caumont

Bayeux

Arromanches

Courseulles

Ouistreham

2nd Br

XII

II Can

I

Caen

1st Can

LXXXVI

II SS

I SS

St Pierre

Villers Bocage

Thury Harcourt

*Vire*

VII

XLVII

LXXIV

*Orne*

Falaise

*Dives*

Condé

Panzer Group West

Granville

Villedieu

Vire

VIII

LXXXIV

*Sée*

Flers

Argentan

Avranches

Pontaubault

Mortain

*Sélune*

XXV

7th

Domfront

St Malo

**British 5.5in. (140mm) medium gun firing in support of Operation *Bluecoat* north of the River Orne. This type of gun fired a 45kg shell to a maximum range of 14,800 metres. Each medium regiment had 16 of these guns. (Imperial War Museum, B9174)**

# ORIGINS OF THE BATTLE

History has shown that the Allied landings in Normandy on 6 June 1944, Operation *Overlord*, were a great success. A firm lodgement was gained by British, Canadian and American forces that day, which the Germans proved incapable of eliminating. The landings were achieved with fewer casualties than had been expected, enemy resistance was lighter than had been feared, and the Allies proved capable of building up men and materiél within the beachhead faster than the enemy's ability to move his forces against the landings. None of the original D-Day objectives were achieved on the day, however, and the strategically important city of Caen remained in enemy hands. Furthermore, the Allied forces were slow in expanding their lodgement, with none of the Allied team willing to risk losing the initiative, or worst still, being evicted from Normandy. Most of the first few weeks were, therefore, spent containing the inevitable German counterattacks against the lodgement and building up a firm base of supplies and manpower.

The Allies then implemented the next stage of *Overlord*. For the Americans this entailed the capture of Cherbourg and the clearing of the Cotentin Peninsula. For the British, the thorny problem of the capture of Caen and an advance onto the flat ground before Falaise dominated their thinking. Montgomery, Commander British 21st Army Group, knew that such an offensive against Caen by his forces would attract fierce resistance from the enemy, for a breakthrough there into what was good tank country would leave the road open to Paris and the whole of northern France. Montgomery's efforts did indeed attract the bulk of German Panzer forces that were moving into Normandy against the landings. Set piece attacks by the British to take the city of Caen or to outflank it were all halted by German armour with little new ground taken and a heavy toll of casualties suffered. Caen did not fall until 9 July, and even then the southern part of the city and the gateway to the Falaise plain was still held by the enemy.

Cherbourg was captured on 27 June by the Americans and they finally cleared the Cotentin Peninsula two days later. General Omar Bradley's forces were then embroiled in bitter fighting amid the thick *bocage* countryside of Normandy, where small fields, sunken lanes, steep banks and high hedges created a dense patchwork of natural defences that the Germans used to full advantage. Advances were measured in yards through countryside almost impenetrable to

**American infantry checks out a dead German soldier on the outskirts of St Lô. The fighting to capture the town was among the worst that US First Army endured during the entire Normandy campaign. (US National Archives)**

Tiger tank from 101st SS-Heavy Tank Battalion (schwere SS-Panzer Abteilung 101). The battalion was in action in Normandy throughout the whole of the campaign. This tank was from Michael Wittmann's 2nd Company. (Bundesarchiv, 1011-738-0217-18)

Armourers arming a Spitfire IX with a 250lb bomb under each wing and a 500lb bomb under the centreline. The aircraft is being prepared for a sortie from an airfield in Normandy in support of ground troops. (Imperial War Museum, CL723)

tanks. Bradley's next goal was the town of St Lô, which was to be used as a springboard for the Americans' great breakout battle, Operation *Cobra*, with the aim of propelling their forces into Brittany and on to the River Loire.

The struggle to overcome the German *bocage* defences and seize St Lô lasted a gruelling five weeks, with the ruins of the town not falling to the Americans until 18 July. Further to the east in the British sector, Montgomery's set piece battles to secure the whole of Caen and manoeuvre on to the flat land to the south-east continued with a great armoured attack, Operation *Goodwood*, in which he hoped to break through onto the Falaise road. *Goodwood* ground to a halt after two days with only minimal gains and the loss of over 400 tanks. These heavy Allied material losses finally led Hitler to consider the possibility that the Allied landings in Normandy were their main effort and that further large-scale landings in the Pas de Calais region were unlikely. As a result,

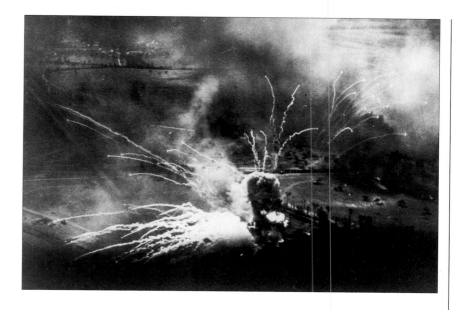

some of the divisions held in reserve by German Fifteenth Army in the Calais area were released and sent to Normandy.

By the end of July the situation in Normandy was gradually turning in favour of the Allies. Since the beginning of the month there had been no doubt that the lodgement was too strong for the enemy to eliminate, but now the time had come to begin a breakout. Montgomery continued his strategy of drawing the bulk of the enemy's armoured formations over to the British sector to weaken those forces facing the Americans in the west. Throughout July Monty ordered Lieutenant-General Dempsey's Second Army to continue with its offensives, both large major operations and smaller repositioning attacks, to tie down German tank divisions. Towards the end of July Bradley was ready to launch his big attack to shatter the German line in the west.

Once Operation *Cobra* was under way, Montgomery would attack simultaneously with both Second Army and the newly organised Canadian First Army, commanded by General Henry Crerar, to prevent the enemy switching his armour across to counter the Americans. Montgomery knew these would be grinding, attritional battles against the substantial Panzer forces facing him, but there was a hope that the massive pressure being applied along the whole of the line might enable the British to achieve a breakout of their own.

# CHRONOLOGY

## 1944

**25 July** General Omar Bradley's US First Army launches its long awaited attack to break the German line, Operation *Cobra*, which begins with a massive carpet-bombing raid on enemy positions. This is followed by a ground attack by US VII Corps. Enemy forces collapse under the weight of the American attack and by the next day are being pushed aside by the armour of US VIII Corps.

**27 July** American forces break right through the German line and achieve a penetration of ten kilometres (six miles).

**30 July** US 4th Armoured Division seizes the town of Avranches, and then captures the bridge at Pontaubault intact the next day, opening the route into Brittany.

**30 July** Montgomery launches Operation *Bluecoat* with VIII and XXX Corps attacking southwards towards Vire from the western side of the British line. Good progress is made by LtGen O'Connor's VIII Corps and a clean breakthrough is achieved, but progress gradually slows as German C-in-C, Generalfeldmarschall Günther von Kluge, shifts three Panzer divisions into the area to halt the attack. On the eastern flank, XXX Corps, performance is disappointing and Montgomery later replaces both the corps commander, LtGen Gerard Bucknall, and the commander of 7th Armoured Division, MajGen George Erskine.

**1 August** US Third Army becomes operational under Gen George Patton and is launched through the Avranches gap into Brittany and southwards towards the River Loire.

**3 August** Hitler orders von Kluge to assemble a strike force of Panzer divisions to attack towards Mortain and Avranches, cutting off those American formations that have advanced southwards towards the Loire and into Brittany.

**4 August** The German line in front of the British is shortened when von Kluge pulls out his Panzer divisions and replaces them with infantry prior to the start of the Mortain offensive. The new line now runs from the River Orne at Thury Harcourt, through Vire,

A group of German NCOs lead a party of prisoners into Canadian lines. Two of the men at the front wear the Infantry Assault Badge (rifle, eagle and oak leaf laurel) on their left breast. This decoration was awarded to troops who had taken part in three successful attacks on three different days. (Harold G. Aikman/National Archives of Canada, PA-116509)

LEFT An American 81mm M1 Mortar firing in support of an infantry attack in Normandy. The mortar had a minimum range of 100 metres, a maximum range of over 3,000 metres and could fire a 3kg bomb. (US National Archives)

RIGHT A convoy from a Canadian field artillery regiment sends up clouds of dust as it passes through the rubble of Falaise on 17 August. The town had been reduced to a ruin by the time Canadian 2nd Division captured it from the Panzergrenadiers of the 12th SS-Panzer Division 'Hitlerjugend'. (Ken Bell/National Archives of Canada PA-145557)

American troops being welcomed as liberators by the French population. Most of the towns and villages captured in the early fighting had been bombed to rubble, but as the German Army began to collapse, whole areas were seized without a fight, much to the relief of the French population. (US National Archives)

The Polish cemetery at Langannerie just to the west of the Caen–Falaise highway, close to where the Polish 1st Armoured Division entered the battle. (Ken Ford)

and then southwards past Avranches. Its realignment allows British XII Corps in the north to advance rapidly across to the Orne south of Caen.

**7 August** Operation *Totalise* is launched by Canadian II Corps after a heavy bombing raid on German defences south of Caen. The Canadians attack along the line of the Caen–Falaise road but are stopped after three days of fighting by a scratch force of II SS-Panzer Corps. Operation *Lüttich*, the German armoured counterattack at Mortain, begins but is almost immediately halted by the Americans with few enemy gains. Further attacks over successive days fail to achieve the breakthrough required by Hitler and the Panzer forces are driven back by the Americans.

**8 August** Patton's forces liberate Le Mans. Bradley orders Patton to turn his XV Corps northward to Argentan to meet up with the Canadians who are pushing southwards towards Falaise to cut off German Seventh and Fifth Panzer Armies in a pocket.

**12 August** Major-General Haislip's XV Corps reaches the outskirts of Argentan and is ordered to halt there to await the arrival of the Canadians. However, as Operation *Totalise* winds up, the latter are bogged down 55 kilometres to the north near Falaise. General Courtney Hodges, now in command of US First Army, and Gen Dempsey, Commander British Second Army, continue to press German Seventh Army from the north and west. Hodges' men take Mayenne and then swing north-east to meet up with US XV Corps to add further pressure on German Seventh Army, commanded by Obergruppenführer Paul Hausser, from the south, while Dempsey's forces strike through the hilly area of the 'Suisse Normande'.

**14 August** Canadian II Corps launches a new attack towards Falaise, Operation *Tractable*. Slow progress is made but Falaise is not reached until 16 August.

**15 August** Lieutenant General Jacob Devers' US Sixth Army Group begins landing forces in southern France in Operation *Dragoon*. Hitler now realises that his forces in Normandy are in danger of being annihilated and orders a general withdrawal to the River Dives. Generalfeldmarschall von Kluge goes missing after his staff convoy is hit by Allied aircraft en route to Hausser's HQ. His mobile signals trucks are knocked out and he remains out of touch with events for a whole day. Hitler suspects something treacherous is afoot and replaces von Kluge with Generalfeldmarschall Walther Model as C-in-C (West).

**16 August** Patton's forces liberate Orléans and reach Chartres two days later.

**17 August** Patton's 79th Division reaches the River Seine and seizes a bridgehead across the river on 19 August.

**18 August** The German escape route from the shrinking Falaise pocket is now confined to the area between Trun and Chambois along the route of the River Dives. The outlook becomes even bleaker for the Germans when Trun is captured by the Canadians and 1st Polish Armoured Division seizes Mont Ormel, leaving it overlooking the German escape route through the valley of the Dives.

US infantry clearing an enemy-held village on the approach to St Lô in early July. The heavy fighting encountered during the fighting for the town slowed down US First Army's advance to a crawl. The same determined enemy resistance to British Second Army's attempts to take Caen led some critics to fear that the battle for Normandy had reached a stalemate. (US National Archives)

**19 August** The Poles link up with Americans in Chambois and close the pocket, but lack sufficient strength to seal it completely.

**Night 19/20 August** Most of the German commanders and troops within the pocket attempt a large-scale breakout. Their escape to the east is blocked by MajGen Maczek's Polish 1st Armoured Division on Mont Ormel and fierce fighting develops.

**20 August** German II SS-Panzer Corps counterattacks towards the gap to help keep it open. Polish 1st Armoured Division is surrounded on Mont Ormel, but supplied from the air holds on in the face of heavy counterattacks.

**21 August** Additional Canadian and American troops arrive to strengthen the cordon between Trun and Chambois and the gap is closed for the last time, finally ending any hope of escape for the surrounded German troops.

**25 August** Paris is liberated and Dempsey's Second Army makes its first crossing of the River Seine at Vernon. The Battle of Normandy is over.

# OPPOSING COMMANDERS

B etween 6 June and the end of July 1944, the Allied team in Normandy remained remarkably intact. No senior officers were removed and replaced even though there was criticism at home regarding the slow progress that the two armies were making in France. In marked contrast to this, during the same period the German Commander-in-Chief (West), GFM von Rundstedt, was replaced, Seventh Army commander, Generaloberst Friedrich Dollmann, committed suicide, and an army group commander (Generalfeldmarschall Erwin Rommel) and an army commander (General Geyr Freiherr von Schweppenburg) replaced due to injuries suffered in Allied air attacks. Before the battle for Normandy was finally over, another Commander-in-Chief (West) (von Kluge) was replaced, later committing suicide, an army commander (Hausser) was wounded by shell fire and another army commander (Eberbach) captured by the British. Normandy was a very dangerous posting for Germany's senior commanders.[1]

## ALLIED COMMANDERS

The Allied Supreme Commander, **General Dwight D. Eisenhower**, maintained overall control of the Allied effort in Normandy. Direction of the campaign on the ground was the responsibility of **General Sir Bernard Law Montgomery** as commander of 21st Army Group. His two army commanders, **General Sir Miles Dempsey** (British Second Army) and **General Omar Bradley** (US First Army) led the British and American contingents. All of these commanders had brought with them a wealth of experience from campaigns in North Africa, Sicily and Italy. Most of their corps and divisional commanders had likewise seen extensive action in those campaigns.

For two months the lodgement in Normandy was too small an area in which to employ more than two armies. As more ground was taken and the German armies were worn down by a war of attrition, Eisenhower began to assemble more and more troops ready for the breakout. These were to be contained in two new armies, which were to become operational once room to deploy them had been won.

**General Sir Bernard Montgomery with his army, corps, and divisional commanders in Normandy. Front row (left to right) MajGen Thomas (43rd Div), LtGen Bucknall (XXX Corps), LtGen Crerar (Canadian First Army), Gen Montgomery (21st Army Group), LtGen Dempsey (British Second Army), Air Vice Marshal Broadhurst (83 Group, 2TAF), LtGen Ritchie (XII Corps). Second row (left to right) MajGen Bullen Smith (51st Div), MajGen Keller (Canadian 3rd Div), MajGen Graham (50th Div), MajGen Roberts (11th Armoured Div), LtGen O'Connor (VIII Corps), MajGen Barker (49th Div), LtGen Crocker (I Corps). Back row (left to right) MajGen Macmillan (15th Div), MajGen Gale (6th Airborne Div) and MajGen Erskine (7th Armoured Div). (Imperial War Museum, B5916)**

---

1 For additional information on the German and Allied commanders in the Normandy theatre during this period, see Campaign Series volumes 100 *D-Day 1944 (1) Omaha Beach*, 104 *D-Day 1944 (2) Utah Beach and the US Airborne*, 105 *Sword Beach and the British Airborne*, 112 *Gold & Juno Beaches*, 88 *Operation Cobra 1944*, and 143 *Caen 1944*.

**Lieutenant-General George S. Patton Jr.** was to command US Third Army, which was brought to Normandy ready to exploit the American breakout into Brittany and north-west France. The 59-year-old Patton was one of America's most famous generals, having won an impressive reputation as an aggressive commander in Tunisia and Sicily. During his early career he had taken part in General Pershing's punitive expedition against Mexico in 1916 and stayed with the general as his ADC in France in 1917. Patton led the US Army's first tank engagement in the World War I with 304th Tank Brigade. Between the wars he was one of the early pioneers of tank warfare and rose to command 2nd Armored Division in 1940. He headed the Western Task Force in the Torch landings in Morocco, commanded US II Corps in Tunisia and helped to plan the invasion of Sicily. Here Patton commanded US Seventh Army and demonstrated his reputed vigour and aggression, but also displayed some of his less admirable traits. In two incidents he 'slapped' American servicemen in military hospitals suffering from battle fatigue. He was passed over by his superior, Eisenhower, in favour of Omar Bradley as commander of the US land forces in the *Overlord* invasion of France. He did later redeem himself in the eyes of the Allied Supreme Commander and was once again given an army command.

As Patton's Third Army became operational, Gen Bradley would be promoted to command of US Twelfth Army Group, with US First and Third Armies under his direct command. Taking over US First Army from Bradley at that point would be **General Courtney Hodges**, a West Point class mate of Patton's. Hodges had entered the army as an infantry private in 1906 and was commissioned three years later. During World War I he rose to command an infantry battalion. He remained in the service after the armistice and spent the next 20 years climbing slowly up the chain of command in the USA until he made Lieutenant General in February 1943. He then headed HQ Third Army preparing it for operational service in France. In early 1944 he arrived in England as Bradley's deputy in US first Army. He had not seen active service since World War I but had proved himself an able if unassuming administrator.

The Canadian **Lieutenant-General Henry Crerar** was to command Montgomery's other army in north-west Europe, Canadian First Army. Crerar had served as an artillery officer in World War I, rising to the rank of lieutenant-colonel. Between the wars he helped build and train

**LtGen George Patton Jr (left),
LtGen Omar Bradley (centre) and
Gen Sir Bernard Montgomery,
(right)** in jovial conversation after
Monty had presented medals to a
number of American officers on
6 July. Relations between these
generals were often very
strained, sometimes bordering
on outright hostility as the
campaign progressed. (Imperial
War Museum, B6551)

RIGHT **MajGen Charles Foulkes, Commander Canadian 2nd Division**, with his ADC in his armoured car in Falaise. Foulkes was later sent to Italy in November 1944 to command Canadian I Corps, then returned with the corps to Holland in February 1945 to join Canadian First Army. (Michael M. Dean/National Archives of Canada, PA-132732)

FAR, RIGHT **Senior commanders of 21st Army Group:** LtGen Courtney Hodges (US First Army), LtGen Henry Crerar (Canadian First Army), Gen Bernard Montgomery, LtGen Omar Bradley (US 12th Army Group) and LtGen Miles Dempsey (British Second Army). Although Bradley commanded his own army group after 1 August, Montgomery still retained overall control of land forces until the end of the battle of Normandy when the Allied Supreme Commander Gen Eisenhower moved his headquarters to France. (Imperial War Museum, B9473)

MajGen J. Lawton Collins, Commander of US VII Corps, which undertook the main effort in Operation *Cobra*. Collins had received the nickname 'Lightning Joe' during his service on Guadalcanal in the Pacific. The name was derived from the shoulder patch of the 25th 'Tropic Lightning' Division which he commanded. (Imperial War Museum, 5919)

Canada's small volunteer army. Crerar later held divisional and corps command in World War II during periods of training, but had had only two months' battle experience as head of Canadian I Corps in Italy in February and March 1944 before he took command of Canadian First Army. Crerar's army contained only one Canadian corps, its II Corps, the remainder of its troops being British and Polish.

# GERMAN COMMANDERS

During the Normandy fighting, Hitler was not only titular head of the German Army, but also exercised great power over all major, and often minor, decisions regarding the conduct of the campaign. The dictator's continual interference in the strategy and tactics in Normandy led to a feeling of impotence in German High Command in the field. **Generalfeldmarschall Hans Günther von Kluge** was Commander-in-Chief (West) and was responsible to Oberkommando der Wehrmacht (OKW) in Berlin, but this in effect meant that he was answerable to Hitler himself. Von Kluge had had a long military career and was among the top five generals of the Army List when war broke out in 1939. He had served in World War I and had remained a career officer rising to Generalleutnant in 1935 and full General der Artillerie the following year. He fought in the Polish campaign, in France and later in Russia with his 4th Army where he gained a strong reputation as a sound and shrewd strategist. He was promoted to Generalfeldmarschall in 1940.

Von Kluge was continually frustrated in Normandy by Hitler's insistence that no ground be given up and refusal to allow even tactical withdrawals. Both von Rundstedt and Rommel had previously incurred the Führer's wrath by suggesting that Normandy should be abandoned and a new line based on the Seine established. Behind this shorter line, the Panzer divisions could be grouped and used in their correct role as a mobile strike force rather than forced to act in a practically static defensive role holding the overextended line in Normandy. When, on 19 July, Army Group B's commander GFM Rommel was wounded by British fighters, von Kluge also assumed direct responsibility for this formation in addition to his role as C-in-C (West). Army Group B included German Fifteenth Army, still based around Calais and in the Low Countries, together with Seventh Army and Panzer Group West in Normandy. This

ABOVE, LEFT **Generalfeldmarschall Günther von Kluge who took over as Commander-in-Chief (West) from von Rundstedt in early July. Von Kluge had commanded 4th Army in France and Russia, then replaced Bock in command of Army Group Centre on the Eastern Front. Von Kluge performed extremely well in Russia and became one of Hitler's favourite field commanders. Von Kluge's handling of the Normandy battle and his loose association with the conspirators of the 20 July plot on the Führer's life led Hitler to lose confidence in him and he was relieved of his command on 16 August and summoned to return to Berlin. He committed suicide en route. (Bundesarchiv, 183-2004-0524-500)**

ABOVE, RIGHT **SS-Obergruppenführer Paul Hausser, Commander German Seventh Army. Hausser was the first SS general to command an army and took over in Normandy against the wishes of both GFM Rommel and GFM von Rundstedt. Nevertheless, he was well respected as a result of his performance in Russia and was regarded by Guderian as one of the outstanding German commanders of the war. He was wounded during his escape from the encirclement south of Falaise, but later returned to command Army Group G towards the end of the war. (Bundesarchiv 146-1977-093-33)**

**General der Panzertruppen Heinrich Eberbach, who had commanded Panzer Group West since early July. While a colonel on the Eastern Front, his tanks advanced over 128 kilometres in a day to capture Orel from the surprised Russians. (Bundesarchiv, 146-1976-096-08)**

brought him closer to the fighting in Normandy and gave him direct control of Seventh Army and Panzer Group West.

**SS-Obergruppenführer Paul Hausser** was given command of German Seventh Army, at the age of 64, on the death of Generaloberst Friedrich Dollmann in early July. A former general in the Imperial army, Hausser had retired from service in 1932 with the rank of Generalleutnant. In 1933, when the forerunner of the Waffen-SS the SS-Verfügungstruppe was being formed, Hausser joined Himmler's new organisation to take charge of training. In 1941 he assumed command of the SS-Division (motorised) 'Reich' in Russia, and was wounded later that year, losing an eye. He later commanded the II SS-Panzer Corps on the Eastern Front and took part in the great tank battle at Kursk. He gained an impressive reputation in Russia and even had the temerity to withdraw his surrounded corps from Kharkov against Hitler's orders. He redeemed himself by retaking the city with the same troops four weeks later. In June 1944 he was in Normandy leading II SS-Panzer Corps against the British. Both von Rundstedt and Rommel opposed his elevation to command of Seventh Army, arguing that such a post should be filled by a regular Wehrmacht general. Hausser was

SS-Obergruppenführer Josef 'Sepp' Dietrich, Commander I SS-Panzer Corps, was an old comrade of Hitler from the days of the Munich beer halls. He was a brave and belligerent general eager to obey the orders of his Führer, but later became disillusioned with Hitler's conduct of the battle in Normandy. (Bundesarchiv, 183-J06632)

the first SS officer to command a German field army. His performance in Normandy justified Hitler's decision to promote him and, despite being severely wounded in the face by a shell fragment during the Falaise fighting, he went on to command Army Group G at the end of the war. Guderian described him as one of the most outstanding of the wartime commanders.

**General der Panzertruppen Heinrich Eberbach** commanded Panzer Group West (later renamed Fifth Panzer Army) in Normandy. He succeeded Geyr Freiherr von Schweppenburg in control of most of the Panzer divisions facing the Allies in France. Eberbach was an officer cadet in World War I, rising to the rank of Oberleutnant attached to the Turkish general staff. After the war he left the army and joined the police. In 1935 he rejoined the Panzer troops of the Wehrmacht and had risen to command 35th Panzer Regiment by the outbreak of World War II. He later fought in Russia and rose from the rank of Oberst to full general in four years!

**SS-Obergruppenführer Josef 'Sepp' Dietrich** commanded I SS-Panzer Corps during most of the fighting, but later rose to command Fifth Panzer Army towards the end of the Normandy fighting. He had been fighting against the invasion since D-Day. He was one of Hitler's oldest companions, one of the first Nazi stormtroopers. He served in World War I as an enlisted man and rose to the equivalent rank of sergeant-major. Dietrich was a rough and ready soldier with more that a touch of the 'bully boy' about him. His rise in the Nazi hierarchy was mainly due to his close association with Hitler – bodyguard and chauffeur – and his ability to carry out his leader's wishes. He took part in the purge of Ernst Röhm's SA Brownshirts in June 1934, during the 'Night of the Long Knives' and was involved in the summary executions of many of the SA's senior leaders. Dietrich led the motorised Infantry Regiment 'Leibstandarte Adolf Hitler' in France in 1940 and then in Greece and Russia. The unit earned a formidable combat reputation during the fighting in Russia. In 1944 he brought the I SS-Panzer Corps to France and was in action with the British immediately after the D-Day landings. Dietrich continued to prosper both during and after the Normandy campaign, rising to command Fifth Panzer Army and then Sixth SS-Panzer Army in the Ardennes and Hungary. Dietrich was a great admirer of Hitler, but became a stern critic of his Führer's military abilities towards the end in Normandy. Dietrich's own capabilities as a senior commander also drew criticism, with most of his contemporaries believing he had been promoted beyond his abilities.

Many of the German division and corps commanders in Normandy had acquired a great deal of experience on active service on the Eastern Front and elsewhere. Several of their senior commanders were men of proven ability, including **SS-Obergruppenführer Willi Bittrich**, commander II SS-Panzer Corps, who had fought in Russia with the SS-Division 'Reich' and SS-Panzergrenadier Division 'Hohenstaufen', and **Generalleutnant Fritz Bayerlein**, commander Panzer Lehr Division, who had served on Guderian's staff in Russia and Rommel's in North Africa.

# OPPOSING FORCES

After almost two months of combat with the Allied forces, the German Army in Normandy was reaching crisis point. It was proving to be no match for its modern mechanised American and British adversaries. Although the fighting in Normandy had already demonstrated that the German forces were still capable of determined resistance and certainly had some skill in defensive fighting, the overall quality of the German Army in the West had deteriorated markedly. Although some of Germany's most powerful units had been sent to the Normandy Front in the immediate aftermath of the invasion, many of those units fighting alongside them had suffered as a result of the savage fighting on the Eastern Front. Even those units that had not served in Russia had often seen the best of their personnel and equipment stripped away in desperate attempts to make good the horrendous losses suffered in the East.

## GERMAN FORCES

Generalmajor Ruldolf-Christoph Freiherr von Gersdorff, Chief of Staff of German Seventh Army, cited several reasons for the Germans' failure to match the Allies in Normandy. Firstly, he considered that the operations staff in position on D-Day and the early part of June at army, corps and division level consisted of many over-age officers who were not accustomed to combat. The demand for senior officers on the Eastern Front and in Italy had absorbed the best personnel. General Dollmann and the staff at Seventh Army, for example, had not seen combat since the invasion of France in 1940. They had no practical knowledge of modern armoured warfare and the organisation and practices of their staff had not adapted to the changes in warfare over the last four years. Their reactions to an invasion by a highly mechanised and powerfully supported Allied army were slow and predictable. A programme of replacing many of these unsuitable commanders was begun early in 1944, but was still far from complete by the middle of the summer.

Another important factor was that the overwhelming majority of German infantry divisions were so-called static divisions, mainly formed for coast defence and garrison duties. Their ranks included many second-rate personnel or non-Germans whose loyalty to the Reich was questionable and who were not up to the demands of frontline combat. Their equipment and transport was so inadequate that the units were classified as unfit for mobile warfare. Most of their transport was horse-drawn, even then the artillery regiments of these static divisions often did not have the full complement of draught horses, but were only able to move one battalion at a time with the aid of horse-team units. Gersdorff

Panzerkampfwagen VI Tiger I in France from an SS unit. The Tiger was present in Normandy in relatively small numbers, but its fearsome reputation resulted in Allied soldiers describing virtually every tank that attacked them as being a Tiger. In the foreground is a Volkswagen amphibious car, the Schwimmwagen. It first appeared in Russia in 1942 as a light reconnaissance vehicle capable of dealing with the many streams and rivers that dotted the countryside. (Bundesarchiv, 1011-299-1804-06)

Most Allied casualties in Normandy were as a result of mortar fire. Here the crew of a 15cm German Nebelwerfer 41 are loading the weapon with six 34kg rockets. The Nebelwerfer could discharge six rocket-propelled mortar bombs in ten seconds, and fire three salvos in five minutes. It had a maximum range of almost 7,000 metres. (Bundesarchiv, 1011-299-1821-27A)

A German gun-aimer protects his ears as a Mörser 18 21cm gun fires towards the British lines from its field position east of the River Orne. This heavy artillery piece could fire a 113kg shell a maximum distance of 18,700 metres. The difficulty in transporting a gun of this size made it vulnerable to Allied spotter aircraft and counter battery fire. (Bundesarchiv, 1011-721-0377-37A)

points out that some of the units were equipped with a variety of weapons of foreign manufacture with the corresponding complications for supply of ammunition and spares. Their anti-tank and anti-aircraft equipment was, in Gersdorff's words, 'utterly inadequate, obsolete and unsuited to large-scale combat.'

The overwhelming Allied air superiority was also a key factor in tipping the scales against the German forces in Normandy. The Luftwaffe was unable to play even a modest role in supporting German forces in the fighting. Luftwaffe strength had never recovered from the punishing assault on its airfields and aircraft by Allied air power in the run up to D-Day. In addition, the bulk of what was left of its strength was heavily committed to trying to counter the increasingly intense Allied bombing campaign against the Reich itself. Their mastery of the air allowed the Allied air forces to attack German lines of communication and supply with impunity, compounding the supply crisis that plagued the German Army in France. It also rendered daytime movement by German units all but impossible.

In addition to those units involved in the fighting, a further German infantry corps, XXV Corps, was committed to the defence of Brittany. This corps contained four divisions, but all of these divisions had been obliged to provide troops to Seventh Army, usually reinforced regimental combat teams of between a third and half of their divisional strength. The troops had been diverted to Normandy in July on the basis that a further Allied landing in Brittany was unlikely. The remaining German garrison in Brittany was therefore relieved of its obligation to guard the coastline against invasion. With the weakening of the forces stationed there, OKW directed that the fortified Brittany ports of Brest, St Malo, St Nazaire and Lorient be maintained at a specified level to prevent them falling into Allied hands. The 319th Infantry Division, commanded by Generalleutnant Graf Schmettow, was, however, to be left in position garrisoning the Channel Islands. Repeated requests by Seventh Army for its release were all rejected; Hitler would not willingly give up the one area of British territory that he had conquered.

The two German armies confronting the Allies in Normandy were of entirely different composition. On the western side of the battlefield German Seventh Army contained a preponderance of infantry divisions with few armoured formations. On 24 July, just before the start of the Allied breakout battles, SS-Obergruppenführer Paul Hausser's Seventh Army fielded ten divisions, of which just three were armoured. By contrast, on the eastern side, General der Panzertruppen Eberbach's Panzer Group West (retitled Fifth Panzer Army on 1 August) had 13 divisions, seven of them Panzer formations.

Two months of heavy fighting in Normandy had reduced the strength of all German divisions both in men and matériel. The war on the Eastern Front was consuming manpower and machinery at an unsustainable rate. Further fighting in Italy and the need to garrison all the occupied territories from Norway to Greece also drained resources. Calls for reinforcement and replenishment by von Kluge in Normandy bought little response from OKW because there were just not enough resources to go around. It was proving impossible to replace the losses on all fronts. Every man, tank and gun lost in the fighting in Normandy was being keenly felt.

The paucity of reinforcements and supplies affected the way German units were deployed. Those that were in the line usually fought with remarkable skill and resilience. The front line was often held with static troops with a secondary line manned by stronger forces situated somewhat further back. Allied attacks were invariably followed by determined enemy counterattacks timed to catch the advance just as its troops were beginning to consolidate their gains.

German artillery, while not matching the levels enjoyed by the British and Americans, was efficient and present in sufficient numbers. The presence of Luftwaffe III Flak Corps in Normandy with its large complement of 88mm dual-purpose anti-aircraft/anti-tank guns gave the divisions in the line a superb additional source of fire support, although there was often some heated discussion between the army and the

A PzKpfw V Panther tank with its long 75mm gun pointed to the rear. The Panthers were in Normandy in sufficient quantities to take a heavy toll of Allied armour. It was designed in response to the Russian T-34 medium tank and incorporated similarly sloped armour. The Panther was considered as probably the best of Germany's tanks. (Bundesarchiv, 1011-705-0264-01)

Luftwaffe as to how the guns should be best used. This fire support was supplemented by three brigades of multi-barrelled Nebelwerfer mortars, 7th 8th and 9th Werfer Brigades, which could both heavily disrupt attacking infantry and inflict high casualties.

## ORDER OF BATTLE

### German forces in Normandy and north-west France, July-August 1944

The organisation of corps and divisions within the German Army in Normandy was fluid, with units being switched to different sectors of the line in response to Allied attacks. The order of battle below is therefore a 'snapshot' of the various armies, corps and divisions in Normandy at the start of the Allied breakout battles on 24 July 1944.

C-in-C (West) – Generalfeldmarschall Günther von Kluge

Army Group B – Generalfeldmarschall Günther von Kluge

**German Seventh Army – SS-Obergruppenführer Paul Hausser**
**II Parachute Corps – General der Fallschirmjäger Meindl**
  3rd Parachute Division – General der Luftwaffe Schimpf
  352nd Infantry Division – Generalleutnant Kraiss

**LXXXIV Corps – General der Infanterie Dietrich von Choltitz**
  Panzer Lehr Division – Generalleutnantt Fritz Bayerlein
  5th Luftwaffe Division – General der Luftwaffe Wilke
  17th SS Panzer Division – SS-Oberführer Baum
  2nd SS Panzer Division 'Das Reich' – SS- Oberführer Heinz Lammerding
  91st Airborne Division – Oberst Eugen Koenig
  243rd Infantry Division – Oberst Bernhard Klosterkaemper
  275th Infantry Division – Generalleutnant Hans Schmidt
  353rd Infantry Division – Generalleutnant Paul Mahlmann

**XXV Corps – General der Infanterie Fahrenbacher** (Based in Brittany)
  77th Infantry Division – Oberst Rudolf Becherer
  265th Infantry Division – Generalleutnant Walther Duewert
  266th Infantry Division – Generalleutnant Karl Sprang
  319th Infantry Division – Generalleutnant Graf Schmettow (Based in the Channel Islands)
  343rd Infantry Division – Generalleutnant Josef Rauch
  2nd Parachute Division – Generalmajor Hermann Bernhard Ramcke

**Panzer Group West (Later Fifth Panzer Army) –**
**General der Panzertruppen Heinreich Eberbach**
**LXXXVI Corps – General der Infanterie von Obstfelder**
  711th Infantry Division – Generalleutnant Josef Reichert
  346th Infantry Division – Generalleutnant Erich Diester
  21st Panzer Division – Generalmajor Edgar Feuchtinger
  16th Luftwaffe Field Division – Generalleutnant Karl Sievers

**I SS Panzer Corps – SS-Obergruppenführer Josef Dietrich**
  1st SS-Panzer Division 'Leibstandarte Adolf Hitler' – SS-Brigadeführer Theodor Wisch
  12th SS-Panzer Division 'Hitlerjugend' – SS-Oberführer Kurt Meyer

**II SS Panzer Corps – SS-Obergruppenführer Willi Bittrich**
  9th SS-Panzer Division 'Hohenstaufen' – SS-Oberführer Sylvester Stadler
  10th SS-Panzer Division 'Frundsberg' – SS-Brigadeführer Heinz Harmel
  277th Infantry Divison – Generalleutnant Albert Praum

**XLVII Panzer Corps – General der Panzertruppen Hans von Funck**
  2nd Panzer Division – Generalleutnant Heinrich von Lüttwitz
  276th Infantry Division – Generalleutnant Kurt Badinski

326th Infantry Division – Generalleutnant Viktor von Drabich-Waechter
116th Panzer Division – Generalleutnant Gerhard Graf von Schwerin

*Moving up at that time:*
272nd Infantry Division – Generalleutnant August Schack
271st Infantry Division – Generalleutnant Paul Dannhauser
LXXIV Corps HQ – General der Infanterie Erich Straube

*Arrived in Normandy before the end of the campaign:*
9th Panzer Division – Generalleutnant Walter Scheller
89th Infantry Division – Oberst Roesler
85th Infantry Division – Generalleutnant Kurt Chill
708th Infantry Division – Generalleutnant Hermann Wilck

# ALLIED FORCES

In marked contrast to the woes of the enemy, Allied supplies and reinforcements continued to arrive in Normandy at a prodigious rate. Numbers of new divisions were being trained and equipped in the USA ready for redeployment to Europe and the industrial resources of the two strongest democracies in the world were dedicated to total war with their factories and shipyards producing war materials at a rate the Germans could only dream of. By the end of the campaign 2,052,299 men, 438,471 vehicles and 3,098,259 tons of supplies were landed in Normandy. For the greater part of the fighting in Normandy troop reinforcements were plentiful, but by the end of the battle the British Army was reaching its manpower limits. Its numbers began to decline as the war went on, resulting in the breaking up of divisions to replenish losses in other units. The crisis of American manpower was not reached until much later in the war.

From a purely numerical viewpoint, the Allies were absolutely dominant. Eisenhower had two tactical air forces (RAF 2nd Tactical Air Force and US 9th Air Force) directly supporting his ground forces and could also call on the use of two strategic air forces (RAF Bomber Command and US 8th Air Force). Armoured divisions and brigades had their losses of tanks replenished as required – the British lost over 400 tanks in Operation *Goodwood* but all were almost immediately replaced, keeping the three armoured divisions up to strength. Fuel, ammunition and transport vehicles poured into the expanding Allied beachhead through artificial harbours and along miles of pipelines. The logistical support given to the fighting forces was staggering.

After almost two months fighting in Normandy many lessons had been learnt by both sides. For the enemy, the complete Allied air superiority meant all movement had to be carried out with caution, particularly during the day, and effective camouflage was essential to avoid the attentions of Allied fighter-bombers. Allied forces could move reasonably freely but German ambushes were frequent. The fighting in the close countryside of the *bocage* suited the enemy, who forced the Allies into a slow, ponderous

A preserved Tiger tank, outside Vimoutiers, still guards the spot on the road where it ran out of fuel after its escape from the pocket in August 1944. (Ken Ford)

An American 51mm anti-tank gun in action in the thick Normandy *bocage* near St Lô. The 51mm gun was a direct copy of the successful British 6-pdr anti-tank gun and was widely used in American infantry divisions throughout the war. Its 2.83kg shell could penetrate 70mm of armour at 1,000 metres. (US National Archives)

American M8 Greyhound armoured cars probe their way through a recently captured French village during the break-out. The 7.6-ton M8 Greyhound was the most widely deployed armoured car in the US Army. It had a top speed of 90kph and was armed with a 37mm gun and a ring-mounted .50in. Browning heavy machine gun. The Greyhound also saw service with the British Army. (US National Archives)

advance, with Allied casualty rates similar to those of World War I. The attacking infantry called upon heavy artillery support to blast gaps in the enemy defences, but was often reduced to probing cautiously along each lane and across each field in search of an unseen enemy. All the advantages of air support, artillery and superior numbers often counted for little on a battlefield where visibility was no further than the next hedgerow. The fighting in the centre of the lodgement was an infantryman's war.

The advantage swung further in the Allies' favour with the introduction of two new armies into the action. On 23 July, after the slight gains south of Caen made by Operation *Goodwood* had carved out a little more room for manoeuvre, LtGen Crerar's Canadian First Army was made operational. Initially, Crerar took just British I Corps under command and assumed responsibility for the sector on the eastern flank round Caen, whilst Canadian II Corps remained with British Second Army. A little later Canadian II Corps joined its parent organisation and eventually Crerar's army contained all the Canadian divisions in Normandy, the Polish First Armoured Division and British I Corps.

In the American sector, LtGen George Patton's Third Army became operational on 1 August, combining with US First Army to form US

Twelfth Army Group. General Omar Bradley then assumed command of this new army group and was replaced as commander of US First Army by LtGen Courtney Hodges. Until Gen Eisenhower decided to take direct command, however, Gen Montgomery continued in operational control of both of the Allied army groups in Normandy.

## ORDER OF BATTLE

**Allied forces, Normandy, July–August 1944**

**BRITISH ARMY**[2]

C-in-C 21st Army Group – Gen Sir Bernard Law Montgomery

**British Second Army – LtGen Sir Miles Dempsey**
**British VIII Corps – LtGen Richard O'Connor**
   Guards Armoured Division – MajGen Allan Adair
   11th Armoured Division – MajGen G.P.B. 'Pip' Roberts
   15th Scottish Division – MajGen G.H.A. MacMillan

**British XII Corps – LtGen Neil Ritchie**
   53rd Welsh Division – MajGen R.K. Ross
   49th West Riding Division – MajGen E.H. Barker
   59th Staffordshire Division – MajGen L.O. Lyne

**British XXX Corps – LtGen G.C. Bucknall** (later LtGen Brian Horrocks)
   British 50th Northumbrian Division – MajGen D.A.H. Graham
   43rd Wessex Division – MajGen G. Ivor Thomas
   7th Armoured Division – MajGen G.W. Erskine

**Canadian First Army – LtGen Henry Crerar**
**Canadian II Corps – LtGen Guy Simmonds**
   Canadian 2nd Division – MajGen Charles Foulkes
   Canadian 3rd Division – MajGen Rod Keller
   Canadian 4th Armoured Division – MajGen G. Kitching
   Polish 1st Armoured Division – MajGen S. Maczek

**British I Corps – LtGen John Crocker**
   3rd Division – MajGen L.G. Whistler
   6th Airborne Division – MajGen Richard Gale
   51st Highland Division – MajGen D.C. Bullen-Smith

**US ARMY**[3]

US Twelfth Army Group – Gen Omar Bradley

**US First Army – LtGen Courtney Hodges**
**US V Corps – MajGen Leonard Gerow**[4]

**US VII Corps – MajGen Lawton Collins**
   3rd Armored Division – MajGen Maurice Rose
   1st Infantry Division – MajGen Clarence Huebner
   4th Infantry Division – MajGen Raymond Barton
   9th Infantry Division – MajGen Manton Eddy
   30th Infantry Division – MajGen Leland Hobbs

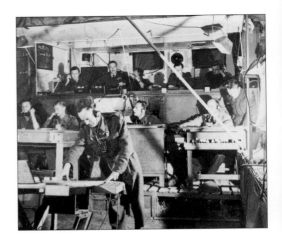

Inside the tented operations room of an RAF Group Control centre in Normandy. Here army and air force personnel work together to direct aircraft on to targets identified by Visual Control Points (VCP) at the front. The VCP usually consisted of an RAF and an army officer in a half-track or scout car up with the leading battalions, relaying back targets requested by the infantry. The army officer was in direct contact with Brigade and the RAF officer with the Group Control Centre. This information allowed sorties by low-flying fighter-bombers to be vectored onto the targets. (Imperial War Museum, CL563)

Tank recovery and repair unit of Royal Electrical and Mechanical Engineers (REME) at 8th Armoured Brigade's workshop. The men are unpacking a new engine for one of the brigade's Sherman tanks. The stencilling on the packing case denotes it was for an M4A1 Sherman, which means that the engine is a Continental R-975 air-cooled radial engine similar to that used in aircraft. (Imperial War Museum, B8888)

**US XIX Corps – MajGen Charles Corlett**
2nd Armored Division – MajGen Edward Brooks
28th Infantry Division – MajGen Norman Cota

*US Third Army – LtGen George Patton Jr*
**US VIII Corps – MajGen Troy Middleton**
6th Armored Division – MajGen Robert Grow
2nd Infantry Division – MajGen Walter Robinson
8th Infantry Division – MajGen Donald Stroh
83rd Infantry Division – MajGen Robert Macon
29th Infantry Division –MajGen Charles Gerhardt

**US XII Corps – MajGen Gilbert Cook**
35th Infantry Division – MajGen Paul Baade
4th Armored Division – MajGen John Wood

**US XV Corps – MajGen Wade Haislip**
79th Infantry Division – MajGen Ira Wyche
5th Armored Division – MajGen S. Leroy Irwin
French 2nd Armoured Division – Général de Division Jacques Leclerc
90th Infantry Division – BrigGen Raymond McLain

**US XX Corps – (MajGen Walton Walker)**
7th Armored Division – MajGen Lindsay McD Silvester
5th Infantry Division – MajGen Stafford Irwin
80th Infantry Division – MajGen Horace McBride

---

2 This is the order of battle during the breakout battles of late July and early August.
3 With the arrival of Third Army in Normandy there was much shifting of divisions between corps and corps between armies during the fluid days of the breakout. Given here is a representation of where the divisions were during the period leading up to the forming of the encirclement and in the drive to the Seine.
4 US V Corps was pinched out of the fighting after *Cobra* and rejoined US First Army during closing of the Falaise-Argentan pocket.

# OPPOSING PLANS

## ALLIED PLANS

The original pre-invasion plan called for Second Army to capture Caen and the wide Falaise plain to the south, while US First Army secured Cherbourg and the Cotentin Peninsula. Then, after a short pause to reorganise, British and Canadian armies would break out towards the Seine and Paris. The Americans would then force their way into Brittany and capture the vital Atlantic ports, before swinging round to the east to come alongside Montgomery's forces. All of these manoeuvres were expected to take place against an enemy that would fall back gradually as superior force was applied to him. There never was any thought of wide-sweeping movements by mobile forces; it was always going to be a long slog.

These plans had to be amended slightly when Dempsey's Second Army failed to capture Caen, being drawn into a long period of very costly fighting trying to take the city. Dempsey drew almost all of the German armour to his sector as Panzer Group West tried to stop the British achieving a breakthrough towards Falaise and the Seine. The enemy saw the British efforts as the main danger and continued to resist Montgomery's attacks on this sector of the line with its most powerful forces. Frustration at being confined to a relatively narrow area led to criticism of Montgomery's methods. This in turn changed the Allies' original policy. Eisenhower came to believe that the main breakout would have to be made in the west. Montgomery's forces now had to attract as much of the enemy strength to the British sector as possible with large, set-piece attacks. Continuously switching pressure back and

PzKpfw VI Tigers of 2nd Company, 101st Heavy SS-Tank Battalion moving up to the front in Normandy just after the invasion. Company commander Hauptsturmführer Michael Wittmann is alleged to be in the lead Tiger, No 205. (Bundesarchiv, 1011-299-1804-07)

forth along the line would force the enemy to maintain powerful forces in the British sector to prevent a breakthrough. By tying down these Panzer divisions, the British would allow the Americans to launch a breakout battle in the west against lighter forces.

This left the infantry of German Seventh Army trying to contain the Americans. After the capture of Cherbourg, Bradley began his moves southwards, attempting to carve out a big enough beachhead to accommodate the many new divisions arriving from the USA. These moves were tenaciously resisted by the enemy, aided by the close countryside of the Normandy *bocage*. Once St Lô had been captured, Bradley planned to launch Operation *Cobra*, an attack on a narrow front with overwhelming force to create a gap that could be exploited by his superior mobile forces. At the right moment he would launch Gen Patton's newly arrived Third Army through the gap and drive into Brittany to capture the Atlantic ports.

While this was taking place at the western end of the line, Montgomery would continue to plug away at Falaise with his new Canadian First Army, all the while threatening to break through to the Seine. Between these two operations, Dempsey's Second Army would push forward to guard the Americans' left flank south of St Lô and engage as many of the enemy as it could. With all of this pressure being applied, von Kluge would have to begin to withdraw his armies towards the Seine. A great opportunity would then open up for the Allies to outflank his forces as they retired north-eastwards across France. Further pressure would be applied to this withdrawal with new landings in the south of France when Gen Jacob Devers' 6th Army Group landed along the Mediterranean coast near Cannes on 15 August. His US Seventh and French First Armies would then advance up the Rhône valley towards the German border against German Nineteenth Army, also threatening to outflank German First Army stationed in central France and along its Atlantic Coast.

Eisenhower's ground forces would be supported every step of the way by RAF 2nd Tactical Air Force and US Ninth Air Force. These both contained ground-support fighter-bombers able to strike individual targets as small as a single tank or vehicle as well as medium bombers to attack larger targets and built-up areas. Eisenhower could additionally

call on the support of the heavy strategic bombers of RAF Bomber Command and US Eighth Air Force. Their Lancaster, Halifax, Flying Fortress and Liberator bombers could carpet bomb wide tracts of land prior to major operations, to saturate enemy positions with high explosive. The employment of these strategic aircraft was a source of controversy, however. They had a poor reputation for accuracy and were involved in numerous 'friendly fire' incidents. The leaders of both these air forces, Air Chief Marshal Arthur Harris and LtGen Carl Spatz, were both unhappy about using their bombers as a battering ram for the army, feeling that such raids interfered with the strategic bombing programme against German industry, in their view a better use of their aircraft and capable of winning the war in itself.

As the Allies planned their battles to break the German line, they were confident that the enemy lacked any appreciable reserves and knew that almost everything he had available was already in the front line. The 'Ultra' team at Bletchley Park in England were decoding many of the German radio messages passing between Normandy and OKW and their contents showed that von Kluge's forces were near to collapse. Operation *Cobra* would break through the western flank of the line while Montgomery held the attention of the bulk of German forces in the east. If everything proceeded according to plan, the Germans in Normandy would have to withdraw or face annihilation.

# GERMAN PLANS

Once the Allies had landed in Normandy, the German Army's original plan was to fence them in and then to sweep them back into the sea. When this proved to be impossible, all efforts were then directed just to contain the beachhead while the new V (vengeance) weapons were developed to attack Britain and to demoralise the nation into submission.

It soon became clear in late June to both of the senior commanders in Normandy, Rommel and von Rundstedt, that the Allies were not

ABOVE **The interior of XII Corps' Army Photographic Interpretation Section command vehicle. Officers are studying the latest aerial reconnaissance photographs of German positions on the corps' front. The pictures were just one of the means available to obtain up-to-date information about enemy troop movements and defences. Such advantages were mostly denied to the enemy whose aircraft were rarely able to fly over Allied lines and return safely with any useful data. (Imperial War Museum, B9391)**

ABOVE, RIGHT **American soldiers fighting an infantryman's war amongst the hedges and ditches of the Normandy *bocage*. Visibility was just as far as the next hedge or field, with the enemy dug in just yards away. (US National Archives)**

going to be evicted and that Normandy would have to be abandoned and a new defence line created on the line of the Seine–Yonne rivers. Hitler would not agree to this and demanded that no ground be given up. He insisted that the Allies must fight for every metre of territory it wrested from German troops. German strategic policy in Normandy therefore simply became Hitler's insistence that Normandy be held.

Such intransigence was extremely demoralising for German commanders in the field, as it meant that tactical withdrawals were out of the question. The front line had to remain where it was and every Allied gain had to be countered by an attack to restore the front. These tactics did not require a great deal of military acumen on the part of army commanders, they merely had to hold the line, plug the gaps and switch their forces to resist new pressure points. The severity of the fighting and the constant stress being applied by the Allies meant there was little chance to withdraw and to regroup or to form any sort of operational reserve. From the beginning of July there was never an opportunity for the elite Panzer forces in Normandy to attack en masse. The Panzer commanders, who had developed great skill in armoured warfare in Russia, were unable to employ their commands as mobile strike forces as had been envisaged because they were continually restricted to a practically static defensive role.

Another factor that had a major effect on German plans was the Allied domination of the air, which precluded any large-scale movement of forces in daylight. All German movement of any size had to be undertaken at night. Allied reconnaissance and fighter aircraft kept a close check on German dispositions and quickly logged any movements within the battlezone or towards it from other regions. The element of surprise was therefore removed from German tactical operations, the Allies always being forewarned of any changes in the line. This aerial observation, coupled with the code-breaking efforts of 'Ultra,' gave the Allies prior knowledge of all reinforcement and redeployment of German forces. At almost every turn, von Kluge and his commanders were frustrated in their attempts to outwit the Allies.

# THE FALAISE CAMPAIGN

## THE BREAKOUT BATTLES

General Omar Bradley's Operation *Cobra* was planned to begin the breakout of American forces from the confines of the Normandy lodgement and into Brittany. Intelligence reports suggested that the German divisions facing his army were too weak to halt the onslaught. Bradley intended to use air power to blast open a gap in the line that would immediately be exploited by US VII Corps, using sufficient numbers of infantry to clear the way for the armour. Facing his First Army between St Lô and the sea were six German divisions, including the depleted Panzer Lehr Division, which had been in almost constant action since 8 June.

*Cobra* got off to an inauspicious start on 25 July when the saturation bombing raid by USAAF aircraft hit not only the German defences but also some of the American troops waiting to go into the attack, causing over 600 casualties, including the death of LtGen Lesley McNair. The first day of the operation was slow as the Americans hit the remains of Panzer Lehr. During the second day things improved and further heavy fighting won a much larger penetration. That same day US VIII Corps attacked on the right of VII Corps. Again there were few initial gains, but by the next day the pressure being applied all along the American line caused the enemy to begin to pull back. Two days into the battle VII Corps had fought its way through the German defences and found that

American infantry meet with men of the British 3rd Division to the east of Vire on 10 August. The British are manning a position covering the road and are armed with a Bren light machine gun and a PIAT handheld anti-tank weapon. (Imperial War Museum, B8983)

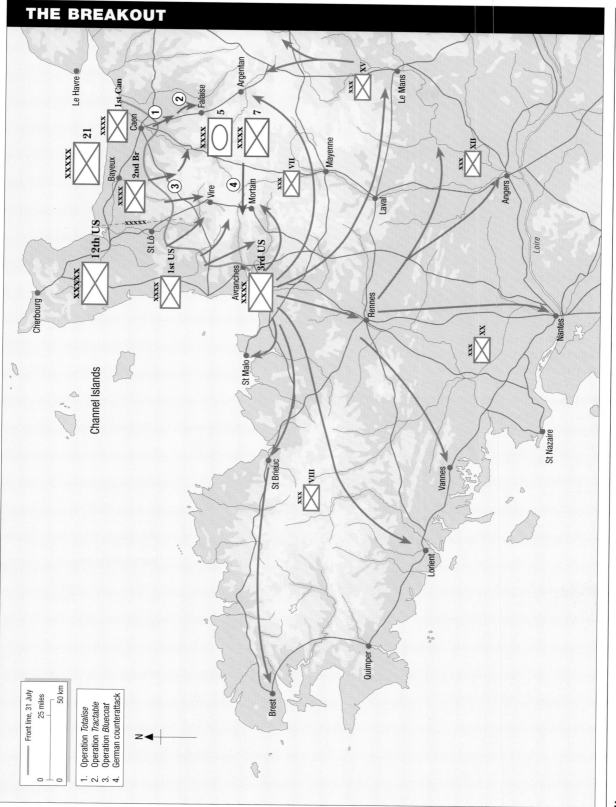

Legend:
- Front line, 31 July
- 0 — 25 miles — 50 km
- 0 — 50 km
1. Operation *Totalise*
2. Operation *Tractable*
3. Operation *Bluecoat*
4. German counterattack

N

Channel Islands

Map labels: Le Havre, 1st Can, Caen, 21, Bayeux, 2nd Br, St Lô, 12th US, 1st US, Cherbourg, Avranches, 3rd US, Vire, Mortain, VII, Mayenne, Laval, Falaise, Argentan, Le Mans, XV, XII, Angers, Loire, Nantes, St Nazaire, Rennes, St Malo, St Brieuc, VIII, XX, Vannes, Lorient, Quimper, Brest

there was little behind them. US 2nd Armored Division was now fed into the breach and began to fan out to the south, driving down towards Avranches, the gateway into Brittany.[5]

It was clear that the Americans were beginning to carve a sizeable salient into German Seventh Army's front. It was now imperative that Montgomery maintain the pressure on Panzer Group West to prevent von Kluge moving any armoured divisions over to the American sector to counter Bradley's advance. On 27 July, Montgomery called a meeting of his army commanders and issued new orders.

Montgomery told Dempsey and Crerar that the progress made by the Americans meant that the breakout had begun and that operations in the eastern sector of the lodgement now had to be geared to support Bradley's offensive. He reasoned that the enemy still expected the British to break out from Caen and advance south-eastwards and had in fact located all six of Panzer Group West's armoured divisions to the east of Noyers. He therefore proposed that a new attack be made in strength to the west of Noyers to tie down German divisions and keep abreast of the left flank of US First Army. Montgomery ordered that British Second Army regroup by bringing VIII Corps into the right of the line next to the Americans and make an attack southwards from the area of Caumont. Montgomery urged that the operation be launched as soon as possible: 'Step on the gas for Vire,' he told Dempsey.

Throughout 28 and 29 July, Dempsey's corps organised a complicated repositioning of their forces which allowed LtGen O'Connor to bring his VIII Corps into the line alongside the Americans to the west of Caumont. The British line was now held, from west to east, by VIII, XXX, XII, Canadian II and I Corps.

East of the River Orne, British I Corps was content to hold the ground won by 6th Airborne Division in June and Operation *Goodwood* in July. South of Caen, Canadian II Corps sat astride the road to Falaise, facing the heavy weight of some of Eberbach's elite Panzer formations. Further to the west British XII Corps' line ran along the route of the Odon and Hill 112, covering ground that was seized at great cost during Operation *Epsom* and the bloody battles of early July. Next came XXX Corps, which had held the whole territory from the boundary with XII Corps across to the Americans before VIII Corps was inserted into the area to the west of Caumont.

Prior to launching Montgomery's new offensive, which by now was called Operation *Bluecoat*, the British front west of the Orne contained VIII, XXX and XII Corps, holding the line with five infantry divisions (15th, 43rd, 50th, 59th and 53rd), three armoured divisions (11th, Guards and 7th), four armoured brigades and three army groups of

A group of German POWs are marched back to the rear from the area to the south of Mont Pinçon, watched by the crew of a Sexton 25-pdr self-propelled gun. (Imperial War Museum, B8875)

5 For a full account of the Operation *Cobra* campaign please consult Campaign 88 *Operation Cobra 1944*.

artillery. Opposing them the enemy had four infantry divisions (326th, 276th, 277th and 271st), one armoured division (21st) and one heavy tank battalion. Two fresh German infantry divisions and an armoured division were also moving up at that time to strengthen them. This gave the British, on paper, a superiority of three to one in armour and almost two to one in infantry, although in reality all the German formations were understrength and very tired. The British superiority in artillery and air power gave them a further advantage.

To go some way towards counterbalancing this overwhelming superiority, the Germans needed to make full use of the advantageous defensive terrain in which the battle was fought. This was the very worst of the Normandy *bocage*, areas of small fields, sunken lanes, high hedges, tree-covered hills and steep-sided valleys. There were very few metalled roads in the region; most were no more than farm tracks, too narrow for two-way vehicular traffic, flanked by steep banks and ditches making movement off the roads difficult. The area was criss-crossed by streams and rivers that either carved out steep valleys or left marshy tracts of land amongst the scattered woody hillsides. What bridges existed were predominantly too weak to bear heavy vehicles. The River Souleuvre cut across the line of advance and its deep valley presented another formidable obstacle.

The attack was to be made by VIII and XXX Corps together, striking southwards from Caumont into the country between the Vire and the Orne to prevent the enemy using the Mont Pinçon ridge as a pivot on which to organise a methodical withdrawal in front of the Americans' advance. If Dempsey's advance kept pace with Bradley's move on Vire and beyond, then the German positions to the east of the Orne and the south of Caen would eventually become untenable. On the left, XXX Corps would attack with its two infantry divisions. The 43rd Wessex Division would strike towards Point 361 on the western end of the Mont Pinçon ridge and 50th Northumbrian Division would secure Amaye sur Seulles to anchor the eastern flank of the operation. On the right, VIII Corps would begin its attack with 15th Scottish Division seizing Point 309, while 11th Armoured Division secured the area around St Martin des Besaces. Once these objectives had been taken and the enemy's front pierced, the Guards Armoured Division in VIII Corps' sector and 7th Armoured Division in XXX Corps' area would pass through and exploit the breakthrough. At the same time as VIII and XXX Corps were attacking in the west, LtGen Ritchie's XII Corps would continue to apply pressure in the east by pushing towards the River Orne through the Odon sector.

Montgomery did not want to give the enemy any advance warning of the attack and so there was to be no preparatory artillery barrage, nor any air bombardment prior to H-Hour. It was

MajGen 'Pip' Roberts, commander British 11th Armoured Division, visiting the battlefield in his armoured truck during Operation *Bluecoat*. Roberts was one of the youngest divisional commanders of the war. His division was amongst the best performing units of the Normandy campaign. (Imperial War Museum, B9183)

**AMERICAN INFANTRY BACKED BY ARMOUR ATTACK A GERMAN POSITION EMBEDDED IN THE TIGHTLY KNIT NORMANDY COUNTRYSIDE OF THE *BOCAGE* DURING THE FIGHTING AROUND ST LÔ IN LATE JULY** (PAGES 34-35)

The overwhelming strength of US First Army and the staggering firepower supplied by artillery and close-support aircraft began to count for little when its troops entered the thick *bocage*. Progress was severely limited by the the Normandy countryside, comprising small fields and high earth banks topped with hedges and narrow lanes, all surrounded by thick undergrowth and vegetation. Fighting was reduced to small scale assaults against an almost unseen enemy. Every hedgerow housed a German anti-tank gun or machine gun nest and every lane formed an anti-tank ditch. The result was many face-to-face actions in which the attackers often came off worse. An American Sherman tank (1) from US 3rd Armoured Division is attacking the line held by Panzer Lehr Division in the *bocage* near St Lô, supported by American infantry (2) from US 30th Infantry Division. The German position was established along hedgerows in sunken lanes, almost impossible to detect except at very close quarters. American infantry have had to rush a German position from across a small field behind the protection of armour. Attached to the front of the Sherman is a Cullin Hedgerow Device (3). This was an improvised attachment thought up by an American engineer to overcome the problems of trying to get over the high banks that surrounded every field lane. The banks acted as an antitank obstacle to advancing armour which had difficulties driving up and over them, for each time a tank crested a

bank it exposed its vulnerable undersides to the enemy. Cullin's solution was to use German 'Hedgehog' obstacles that littered the landing beaches. These devices were made from pieces of railway line welded together to form spikes which were designed to rip the bottom out of landing craft. Sergeant Cullin used the rails to construct a kind of ram which was welded to the front of the tank. In action the tank would drive hard at the bank, the protruding ram would penetrate into the earth breaking up the bank and the device would then burrow through, pushing the earth and roots of the hedge up over the front of the tank. Many types of these Cullin devices were improvised by tank crews and fitters in the field. They often took on a variety of hastily welded shapes and forms. The German 75 mm anti-tank gun (4) had been sited to cover the field to its front, but the sudden rush by American infantry and tanks has given the crew little time to engage all of the attacking armour. One Sherman has managed to get through to the German line and the position is now lost. Some of the enemy try to flee, others are dealt with by the accompanying American infantry. One brave panzer-grenadier (5) is in a position to engage the Sherman tank with a Panzerfaust handheld anti-tank weapon, but from such close quarters he may well perish in the resulting blast. It required a great deal of courage to use these portable weapons. Each country had examples of this type of anti-tank 'bazooka' in their arsenal and their effectiveness all depended on the user getting into a good position close to the armour he was stalking. Not surprisingly, many of those who tried to use them were killed by supporting infantry or by the machine guns of the tanks themselves.

important that the impending offensive be kept secret. The initial advance would be covered by the artillery firing on known fixed defences. As the attack got underway, RAF Bomber Command would bomb four areas 6,000 yards in front of the infantry and US Ninth Air Force would do the same to three areas in front of VIII Corps. Fighter-bombers would be available to strike individual ground targets as the battle progressed.

## Operation *Bluecoat*

Montgomery's breakout battle began at 06.00hrs on 30 July with XXX Corps attacking on a three-brigade front. On the extreme left, 50th Division led the way with 231st and 56th Brigades striking at the junction between the German 326th and 276th Infantry Divisions, with 130th Brigade from the 43rd Division keeping abreast of them to the west. Both attacks were supported by regiments of the 8th Armoured Brigade. VIII Corps began its attack an hour later with 227th Brigade of the Scottish Division and 11th Armoured Division's 29th Armoured and 159th Infantry Brigades attacking on the flank of the Americans as they continued their drive towards Vire.

All along the line the attacking troops were met with very heavy fire and thick minefields. Having held this line for some time, the enemy had had ample time to thoroughly prepare his defences. Royal Engineers had cleared routes up to the start lines and flail tanks from 79th Armoured Division were up with the leading brigades to deal with the obstacles. The scale of the minefields took the Allies by surprise, however, and progress through them was slow with the attacking divisions suffering high casualties.

Thirty Corps met stiff resistance, forcing its progress to a crawl. By the end of the day 50th Division had gained just 1,800 metres. The 43rd Division had captured the village of Briquessard, but had been stopped short of Cahagnes, just five kilometres from the start line. The attack by VIII Corps, which began at 07.00hrs, had fared much better; their leading units had penetrated eight kilometres to the south of Caumont. The Scottish Division had its 227th Brigade in the lead with 6th Guards Armoured Brigade in support and had taken Point 226 by early afternoon. It had been a hard fight – seven of the Guards' Churchills and two flail Shermans had been disabled by mines within a few hundred metres of the start line.

Having achieved a successful penetration, the tanks were urged to push on to Point 309. The Churchills drove straight for the hill; several became bogged down and a few overturned as they rushed up the steep slopes, but by 19.00hrs the leading squadron had reached the summit. The German defenders had fled from the onrushing armour. The tanks beat off enemy attempts to retake the hill with a barrage of machine-gun fire until the infantry joined them just before dark, strengthening the Allied hold on the hill. Meanwhile the Germans began to respond to the penetration. In an enemy counterattack against Hill 226, a squadron of the tank brigade lost a number of tanks to artillery fire and several more to three Jagdpanthers that drove right over the top of the hill. These massive German tank destroyers were engaged by Churchills from the other squadrons. Two Jagdpanthers had their tracks shot off and were abandoned, the other escaped back to German lines. The enemy attack

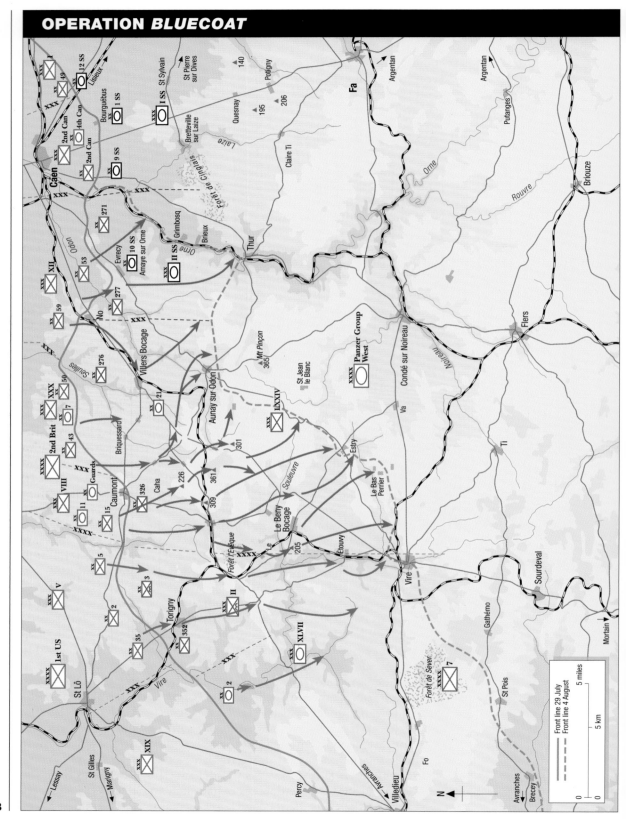

over, more infantry from 15th Division arrived and consolidated the positions on the hill for the night.

Further to the right, 11th Armoured Division had also made good progress advancing on a two-brigade front with 159th Infantry and 29th Armoured Brigades, both groups being a mix of armour and infantry. As elsewhere, the attack began cautiously through thick minefields before penetrating into the enemy positions. The *bocage* then made the going very slow as the tanks and infantry picked their way through small woods and steep valleys raked by enemy fire. Cussy was taken and by nightfall the division was within three kilometres of its first objective of St Martin des Besaces. To its right, the Americans were continuing their drive on Vire, but were lagging slightly behind the British with their V Corps unable to advance further than the St Lô–Caumont road.

The British attack had struck LXXIV Corps head-on and the penetration made by 11th Armoured Division in the west had pushed 326th Division to the east. The armoured division was now passing down the flank of II Parachute Corps, which was resisting the American advance. During the day, II Parachute Corps had lost all touch with 326th Division leaving its flank exposed. Air attacks had put its headquarters out of commission and two of its regimental HQs were under attack by British tanks. Generalfeldmarschall von Kluge received this news with concern, and decided to commit his only armoured reserve against the British penetration. At 17.00hrs he ordered the under-strength 21st Panzer Division to move across to the Caumont sector. He also agreed to allow II Parachute Corps to withdraw during the night to new positions running westwards from St Martin des Besaces to protect its exposed right flank. Cracks were starting to appear in the German line.

The next day, 31 July, 50th Division continued its slow drive towards Amaye sur Seulles against heavy opposition from German 276th Division. It made little progress in the thick *bocage*. To its right 43rd Division took most of the day to capture Cahagnes and St Pierre du Fresne. LtGen Bucknall then decided to swing behind the opposition in front of 50th Division by introducing his 7th Armoured Division into the battle and sending it south-eastwards towards Aunay sur Odon. Unfortunately, the absence of any good roads running in that direction forced the armoured division to seek a route through Caumont and it became entangled in massive traffic jams, as the tail of 43rd Division had not yet cleared the town. By nightfall, against negligible opposition, 7th Armoured Division had pushed forward no more than eight kilometres to Aunay sur Odon. XXX Corps was not performing at all well.

On VIII Corps' front, progress continued to be good. The Scottish Division extended its position south of Point 309 and dealt with the arrival of 21st Panzer Division on the battlefield. The German armour attempted to concentrate several times during the morning in preparation for an attack against the 15th Division. On each occasion it was bombed by Allied aircraft and shelled by British artillery. Five squadrons of RAF 83rd Group Typhoons harassed the Panzers all morning, claiming 30 tanks destroyed. Nonetheless, the presence of German tanks supported by infantry to their front, was an unwelcome development for 15th Division, but the Scotsmen were able to hold their positions.

On the offensive's western flank MajGen 'Pip' Roberts' 11th Armoured Division had a very good day. Its tanks captured St Martin des

Besaces in the morning, while the armoured cars of the Household Cavalry probed further to the south towards the River Souleuvre, passing through the Evêque Forest and the village of La Ferrière against only light opposition. Throwing caution to the wind they pressed on towards the river, eight kilometres in front of the rest of the division. At around 10.30hrs the leading squadron found an intact and unguarded bridge over the Souleuvre. A radio message was swiftly relayed back to brigade; tanks and more armoured cars were despatched to secure a bridgehead over the river and by late morning Roberts was ordering more tanks and infantry across. The 11th Armoured Division took Hill 205 south of the bridge and established itself in force just three kilometres to the west of Le Beny Bocage and seven miles short of Vire.

The 11th Armoured Division was causing yet more problems for German II Parachute Corps, whose right flank was once more exposed. US V Corps, taking advantage of the German withdrawal the night before, was also piling on the pressure. Moving up fast alongside the British, it was now just five kilometres behind them close by the western edge of the forest. With a bridge over the Souleuvre, LtGen O'Connor now introduced the Guards Armoured Division into the battle to the left of 11th Armoured Division. Its advance was not as rapid, meeting heavy German resistance from elements of 21st Panzer Division around Point 192 just to the south of St Martin de Besaces and forced to halt for the night.

The next day, 1 August, the offensive continued. The 11th Armoured Division took Le Beny Bocage and pressed on to within three kilometres of Vire. Resistance here stiffened and the division halted its advance as Vire had been transferred to the American sector and was now the responsibility of US V Corps. The Guards Armoured Division captured Point 192 and then Le Tourneur before seizing another bridge over the Souleuvre. In the meantime, both VIII Corps' 15th Scottish Division and XXX Corps' 43rd Division continued to resist counterattacks by the 21st Panzer Division. Further to the east, 50th Division finally took Amaye sur Seulles, but 7th Armoured Division made little further progress towards Aunay sur Odon.

German 21st Panzer Division's attempts to counter the Allied advance and retake Point 309 had been stopped by overwhelming British force. The German division's left flank was becoming more exposed by the hour as 11th Armoured Division pushed southwards. Panzer Group West's commander, Gen der Panzertruppen Eberbach, realised that LXXIV Corps' sector was now the critical point on the entire front. A British breakthrough here might well cut off Seventh Army and tear open the whole line. He now urged von Kluge to give permission for him to reinforce the Caumont sector with additional Panzer troops, arguing that, important though the area east of the Orne was, the battle south of Caumont was crucial for the whole German front in the west. After lengthy discussion the C-in-C (West) agreed and authorised the transfer of II SS-Panzer Corps[6] from south of Caen into the line alongside II Parachute Corps. The corps was also to take command of 21st Panzer Division, thus placing three armoured divisions across British Second Army's line of advance. II SS-Panzer Corps was ordered to halt 7th

---

6 9th SS-Panzer Division 'Hohenstaufen', 10th SS-Panzer Division 'Frundsberg', 8th Werfer Brigade and 668th Heavy Tank Battalion.

A tank crew from 13th/18th Royal Hussars man a slit trench on the road leading to Mont Pinçon on 8 August. Their tank had been knocked out by a mine and they are acting in the role of infantry while waiting for a tank recovery unit to come to their aid. (Imperial War Museum, B8852)

Armoured Division's thrust towards Aunay sur Odon with 10th SS-Panzer Division 'Frundsberg', whilst 9th SS-Panzer Division 'Hohenstaufen' eliminated the British bridgeheads over the Souleuvre and re-established secure contact with II Parachute Corps at Carville.

On 2 August, Gen Dempsey's advance continued. VIII Corps pushed the 11th and Guards Armoured Divisions further southwards occupying the Perriers Ridge overlooking the Vire–Vassy road. Progress was initially good, but resistance increased dramatically as the day wore on when the leading units of 9th SS-Panzer Division arrived in the area. The pressure from the British, however, prevented the Panzer units grouping for a decisive attack and they were forced to react to the British penetrations along the whole of the line.

As Vire was no longer an objective, it was decided that VIII Corps should wheel south-eastwards towards Condé sur Noireau and Flers, whilst XXX Corps headed for the River Orne above Thury Harcourt. This shift to the east allowed VIII Corps to add a fourth division into the battle, and 3rd Division was brought across from Caen to enter the line between 11th Armoured and the Americans. O'Connor's attack could now continue on a four-division front.

On the eastern side of Dempsey's attack, XXX corps was still trying to advance through some of the densest countryside in the *bocage*. The Wessex Division advanced about five kilometres and took Jurques and Hill 301, hammering away at 21st Panzer Division and well-entrenched enemy infantry. British 50th Division was still trying to clear the high ground east of Amaye sur Seulles. Between 50th and Wessex divisions, 7th Armoured was still struggling to reach Aunay sur Odon with disappointing results. Successive attacks on 2 and 3 August with its armoured and infantry brigades respectively made little progress. On 3 August 10th SS Panzer Division counterattacked and 7th Armoured was driven right back to Breuil, the village it had captured two days before. This setback was too much for Gen Montgomery. Bitterly disappointed with XXX Corps' lack of progress, he made sweeping changes, sacking XXX Corps' commander, LtGen Bucknall, the commander of 7th Armoured Division, MajGen Erskine and the commander of 22nd Armoured Brigade, Brigadier Hinde.

# CAPTURE OF MONT PINÇON

The 43rd (Wessex) Infantry Divisions attack on the massive feature of Point 365 known as Mont Pinçon. The hill was the highest point along a series of features which formed a formidable obstacle to the Allied advance. The capture of Mont Pinçon was achieved at great cost to the men of Wessex during some of the worst fighting of the whole campaign.

Note: Gridlines are shown at intervals of 1 km/0.62 mile

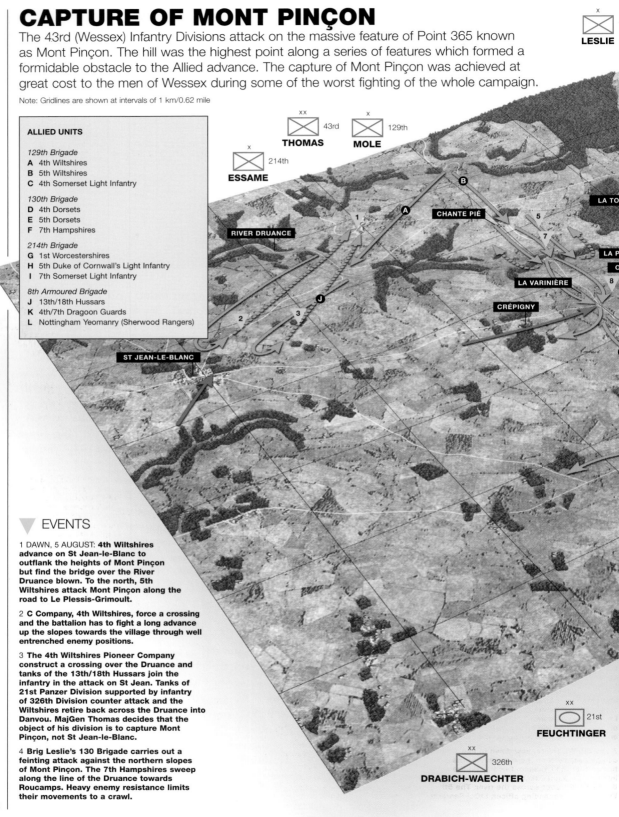

**ALLIED UNITS**

*129th Brigade*
A  4th Wiltshires
B  5th Wiltshires
C  4th Somerset Light Infantry

*130th Brigade*
D  4th Dorsets
E  5th Dorsets
F  7th Hampshires

*214th Brigade*
G  1st Worcestershires
H  5th Duke of Cornwall's Light Infantry
I  7th Somerset Light Infantry

*8th Armoured Brigade*
J  13th/18th Hussars
K  4th/7th Dragoon Guards
L  Nottingham Yeomanry (Sherwood Rangers)

LESLIE

THOMAS — 43rd
MOLE — 129th
ESSAME — 214th

RIVER DRUANCE

CHANTE PIÉ
LA TO
LA P
LA VARINIÈRE
CRÉPIGNY
ST JEAN-LE-BLANC

FEUCHTINGER — 21st
DRABICH-WAECHTER — 326th

## ▼ EVENTS

**1** DAWN, 5 AUGUST: **4th Wiltshires advance on St Jean-le-Blanc to outflank the heights of Mont Pinçon but find the bridge over the River Druance blown. To the north, 5th Wiltshires attack Mont Pinçon along the road to Le Plessis-Grimoult.**

**2** **C Company, 4th Wiltshires, force a crossing and the battalion has to fight a long advance up the slopes towards the village through well entrenched enemy positions.**

**3** **The 4th Wiltshires Pioneer Company construct a crossing over the Druance and tanks of the 13th/18th Hussars join the infantry in the attack on St Jean. Tanks of 21st Panzer Division supported by infantry of 326th Division counter attack and the Wiltshires retire back across the Druance into Danvou. MajGen Thomas decides that the object of his division is to capture Mont Pinçon, not St Jean-le-Blanc.**

**4** **Brig Leslie's 130 Brigade carries out a feinting attack against the northern slopes of Mont Pinçon. The 7th Hampshires sweep along the line of the Druance towards Roucamps. Heavy enemy resistance limits their movements to a crawl.**

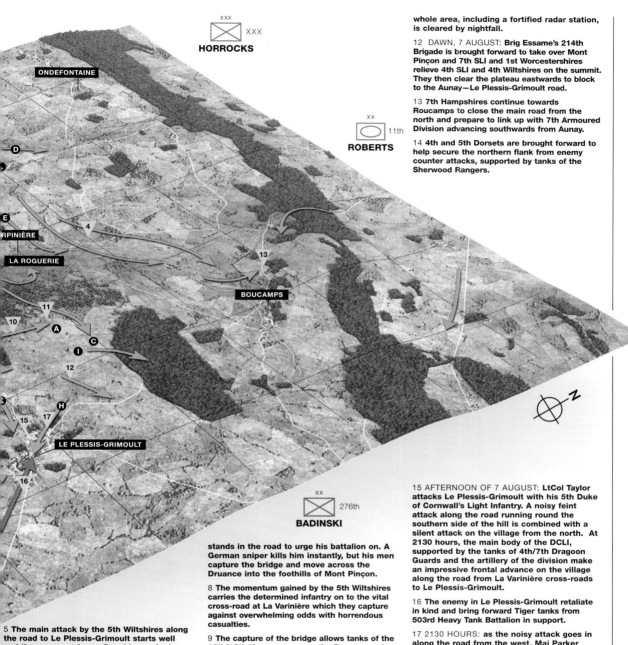

**HORROCKS**
XXX
XXX

ONDEFONTAINE

D

E

RPINIÈRE

LA ROGUERIE

**ROBERTS**
XX
11th

4

13

BOUCAMPS

11

10

A

C

I

12

3

H

15

17

LE PLESSIS-GRIMOULT

16

**BADINSKI**
XX
276th

Z

whole area, including a fortified radar station, is cleared by nightfall.

12 DAWN, 7 AUGUST: **Brig Essame's 214th Brigade is brought forward to take over Mont Pinçon and 7th SLI and 1st Worcestershires relieve 4th SLI and 4th Wiltshires on the summit. They then clear the plateau eastwards to block to the Aunay—Le Plessis-Grimoult road.**

13 7th Hampshires continue towards Roucamps to close the main road from the north and prepare to link up with 7th Armoured Division advancing southwards from Aunay.

14 4th and 5th Dorsets are brought forward to help secure the northern flank from enemy counter attacks, supported by tanks of the Sherwood Rangers.

5 **The main attack by the 5th Wiltshires along the road to Le Plessis-Grimoult starts well and the cross-road near Duval is reached without difficulty. The bridge at the base of the mountain is held in force. Companies that get across the river are withdrawn under cover of darkness after being surrounded.**

6 DAWN, 6 AUGUST: **Brig Mole orders 4th Somerset Light Infantry to advance on the hill along the route leading from La Toque through La Roguerie. The advance is brought to a halt around La Roguerie by accurate machine-gun and mortar fire from enemy on the hills.**

7 The 5th Wiltshires, now down to two companies, try once more to capture the bridge over the Druance. Once again the infantry are pinned down by enemy fire from the wooded slopes across the river. The 5th Wiltshire's commanding officer, LtCol Pearson,

stands in the road to urge his battalion on. A German sniper kills him instantly, but his men capture the bridge and move across the Druance into the foothills of Mont Pinçon.

8 The momentum gained by the 5th Wiltshires carries the determined infantry on to the vital cross-road at La Varinière which they capture against overwhelming odds with horrendous casualties.

9 The capture of the bridge allows tanks of the 13th/18th Hussars to cross the Druance and join up with the leading infantry. The leading Shermans find a small unguarded track leading up to the summit of Mont Pinçon just past the La Varinière cross-roads.

10 A Squadron of the 13th/18th Hussars send an armoured patrol up the track and seven tanks gain the summit of Mont Pinçon and get behind the main line of German resistance on the forward face of the hill. This success is quickly exploited by Brig Mole's third battalion and 4th Wiltshires are ordered up on the summit to consolidate the position held by the tanks.

11 With tanks on the top of Mont Pinçon, the 4th SLI of 130th Brigade fight their way to the top of the high ground and join the Hussars on the broad plateau around its summit. The

15 AFTERNOON OF 7 AUGUST: **LtCol Taylor attacks Le Plessis-Grimoult with his 5th Duke of Cornwall's Light Infantry. A noisy feint attack along the road running round the southern side of the hill is combined with a silent attack on the village from the north.** At 2130 hours, the main body of the DCLI, supported by the tanks of 4th/7th Dragoon Guards and the artillery of the division make an impressive frontal advance on the village along the road from La Varinière cross-roads to Le Plessis-Grimoult.

16 The enemy in Le Plessis-Grimoult retaliate in kind and bring forward Tiger tanks from 503rd Heavy Tank Battalion in support.

17 2130 HOURS: as the noisy attack goes in along the road from the west, Maj Parker leads his A Company of the 5th DCLI silently through the gathering darkness into the northern outskirts of the village. At 2210 hours the barrage stops and Parker's men attack and begin the task of clearing the village. In the darkness, two 69-ton Tiger II tanks (Royal Tigers) from 1 Company 503rd Heavy Tank Battalion enter the village. One is knocked out by a PIAT, the other withdraws southwards to safety. The remaining enemy in the village soon surrender.

18 DAWN, 8 AUGUST: the Wessex Division continue to clear the enemy from the area to the south of the feature, but with the dominant Mont Pinçon now taken and the German line broken, XXX Corps can continue its advance southwards towards Condé-sur-Noireau.

It was a great disappointment that the famed 7th Armoured Division, 'the Desert Rats' one of the British Army's finest divisions, had performed so poorly in Normandy. Montgomery had insisted on bringing the division back from the Mediterranean specifically to take part in the invasion. It included a core of battle-hardened veterans with a wealth of combat experience and it had been assumed that the division would play a leading part in the fighting. The reasons for the division's lack of success were complex, but one factor may have been that her veterans had simply had enough of war. They had seen a great deal of fighting in the Mediterranean theatre and perhaps felt that it was now the turn of others to do their share. The division's new commander, MajGen Verney, succeeded in turning the situation around, however. Additional replacements were fed into the division during the campaign in NW Europe and the 'Desert Rats' went on to win many more battle honours before the war ended.

On 4 August LtGen Brian Horrocks took over XXX Corps. Horrocks was a favourite of Montgomery, having fought in North Africa where he commanded a corps at Alamein and in the subsequent battles. Horrocks was seriously wounded in Tunisia and spent over a year in England recovering from his injuries. The commander was well-liked and respected by his men and superiors alike, who had complete faith in his abilities. Perhaps as important he was a lucky and successful fighting general.

On Second Army's right flank, US First Army continued to make significant progress. Although Vire had not fallen to US V Corps, First Army continued to fight its way south and south-east, grinding down the enemy. Bradley's *Cobra* offensive had driven the German front back to the base of the Cotentin Peninsula around Avranches. By 31 July, as British Second Army pushed south from north-east of Vire in Operation *Bluecoat*, the Americans were poised to break out of Normandy into Brittany. A captured a bridge over the River Sélune at Pontaubault became the channel for the breakout. German Seventh Army's left flank rested on the coast. With the capture of Avranches and Pontaubault, Seventh Army's flank was turned. All that barred the Americans' route south were scattered infantry garrisons in the German rear areas.

On 1 August, Gen George Patton's US Third Army became operational and exploded through this gap into north-western France. This highly mechanised force now fanned out in three directions, urged onwards by its energetic and aggressive commander. First MajGen Troy Middleton's VIII Corps turned west into Brittany, heading for St Malo and Rennes and the Atlantic ports of Brest, Lorient and St Nazaire. It faced little effective resistance as German XXV Corps, defending the peninsula, had withdrawn the bulk of its divisions into the fortresses surrounding the four main ports. Progress was swift and spectacular.

Early on the morning of 3 August, GFM von Kluge received a startling order from German OKW that would lead directly to the utter downfall of the German Army in Normandy. Hitler had decided that the front between Vire and the Orne would be held by infantry divisions, releasing a number of armoured divisions that would be transferred to the left flank. The German forces would withdraw to a new line between Thury Harcourt and Vire, including the high ridge of Mont Pinçon. The assembled Panzer forces would make a concerted attack against the Americans at Mortain, with a view to isolating and destroying those units of US Third Army that had passed through Avranches and were driving

A Kingtiger from 503rd Heavy Tank Battalion knocked out in Le Plessis-Grimault at the base of Mont Pinçon by 5th Duke of Cornwall's Light Infantry. This was one of the first of these 70-ton Tiger IIs to be captured by the British. (Imperial War Museum, B8947)

into Brittany and towards the Loire. Von Kluge immediately recognised the plan as madness, knowing that Allied air superiority and the strength of Allied ground forces would negate such an attack as they had every major German attack since 6 June. He realised only too well that his front was collapsing and, short of reinforcing it with a large number of new divisions, the only sane thing to do was to withdraw Seventh Army and Panzer Group West to a new line based on the River Seine. However, 'Befehl ist Befehl' and he duly gathered his Panzers ready for the attack.

At the same time that the C-in-C (West) was making plans to implement Hitler's latest directive, Montgomery issued a general order to the four Allied armies in Normandy for a broad offensive in the opposite direction. His intention remained to hold firm on the left flank and swinging hard with the right. The British and Canadian armies would continue to absorb the attention of as much of the German armour as possible and press forward to the Orne and Falaise. The Americans, at that very moment sweeping west and south into Brittany and the Loire, would swing east and then north-east towards Paris and the lower Seine. Airborne forces would then be landed ahead of the Americans to secure the Chartres area to aid the advance and to prevent the retreating Germans escaping.

The first effects of Hitler's orders were seen early on the morning of 4 August, as the troops holding the German line south-west of Caen made an orderly withdrawal behind the River Orne as far south as Thury Harcourt. British XII Corps soon discovered that the enemy in front of it was slipping away and pressed forwards through minefields and booby traps with 53rd and 59th Divisions, taking Amaye sur Orne, Evrecy and Villers Bocage, towns the Allies had spent more than two months trying to reach. The next day XII Corps had closed up to the Orne between Caen and the loop of the river north of Thury Harcourt. From here, the front line curved back to the north around the looming heights of Mont Pinçon and then across to VIII and XXX Corps' sector where the line was unchanged. These two corps had continued pressing forwards, albeit at

American 155mm gun being towed forward during the American breakout. This large weapon had its origins in the French 155 GPF gun adopted by the Americans in 1917. Its M1 carriage was designed for high speed and manoeuvrability with pneumatic tyres and air brakes. (US National Archives)

a slow pace against the tanks and infantry of II SS-Panzer Corps. VIII Corps' 3rd Division had to resist repeated attempts by 9th SS-Panzer Division 'Hohenstaufen' to retake Perriers Ridge, and it required determined fighting from 15th Division to make headway towards Vassy against 10th SS-Panzer Division 'Frundsberg'. Between VIII and XII Corps, XXX Corps used 43rd Division to bludgeon its way into Ondefontaine in its advance towards the commanding slopes of Mont Pinçon, while 7th Armoured Division finally entered the now-abandoned Aunay sur Odon, its objective for the past five days. The tired 50th Division was finally pulled out and sent into reserve, the first time since D-Day that it had not been responsible for any part of the front line.

The Mont Pinçon ridge was strategically placed in the centre of Second Army's front. It had long been seen as vital to the enemy's defences, with British planners expecting the Germans to use the great hill as a bastion on which to pivot their line if it was in danger of being forced back to the River Orne. The commanding views obtained from its summit were of great tactical advantage to them.

The 43rd Wessex Division under MajGen Thomas was given the job of capturing Mont Pinçon and no one had any illusions about how difficult a task it would be. The enemy infantry holding the feature were sure to contest every foot of the advance to the hill's base and then resist with great force any attempt to drive them off its summit. Their assumptions were proved correct. The Wessexmen fought an exhausting battle suffering heavy casualties to reach the small stream that ran around the base of the hill. This was the 5th Wiltshires' worst battle of the entire war. They lost their commanding officer killed and most of their remaining officers killed or wounded. The Wiltshiremen fell in droves and other famous West Country battalions suffered almost as badly; the Dorsets, the Hampshires and the Somerset Light Infantry all took a heavy toll of casualties whilst closing on the great feature. Then, almost unexpectedly the battle turned in favour of the 43rd Division when a troop of Shermans from 13th/18th Royal Hussars found an unguarded track and drove without opposition up to the summit. They were quickly reinforced with infantry and within a few hours had secured the plateau on top of the hill and cleared the way for tanks and infantry to move around the hill the next day. The capture of Mont Pinçon was a great blow to the enemy and he had to realign his front quickly to prevent his line being turned.

# THE NET BEGINS TO CLOSE

On 5 August, US XV Corps (MajGen Wade Haislip) pushed through the gap at Avranches and then swung south-east towards Le Mans and the headquarters of Hausser's Seventh Army. It was followed on 7 August by US XX Corps (MajGen Walton Walker), which advanced south towards Nantes and Angers on the River Loire. Once all of Patton's divisions had landed in France, US XII Corps (MajGen Gilbert Cook) also joined in the chase and passed through XX Corps heading for Orléans. Patton personally urged his commanders to drive their men onwards, at one point hustling as many as seven divisions through the bottleneck at Avranches and Pontaubault in 72 hours. The Americans now cut loose into the rear of German Seventh Army.

### The German Counterattack at Mortain

With the lines of supply and communication of all these corps passing through the gap at Avranches, the vulnerability of this narrow channel was not lost to Hitler. Unaware of the realities of the German situation in Normandy, he reasoned that a concerted armoured strike through Mortain towards the sea would cut off Patton's forces to the south and restore Seventh Army's line. The Panzer force could then turn north and drive into US First Army's rear. It was this flawed logic that lay behind the order von Kluge received on 3 August. Unfortunately, the Führer had still not accepted the critical condition of German forces in Normandy or the overwhelming nature of Allied air power. He also

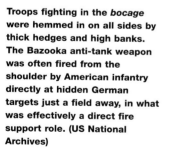

Troops fighting in the *bocage* were hemmed in on all sides by thick hedges and high banks. The Bazooka anti-tank weapon was often fired from the shoulder by American infantry directly at hidden German targets just a field away, in what was effectively a direct fire support role. (US National Archives)

The Germans used a large number of horses in Normandy. Much of the transport for second line and static infantry divisions was horse-drawn, as were the limbers for the guns. The sight of dead horses became commonplace during the campaign and added to the stench of decay that hung over the battlefield. (US National Archives)

The rapid advances made by US Third Army against almost negligible opposition led to a feeling of euphoria amongst American servicemen. Here a group of infantry are happy to show off their trophies seized from captured Germans. (US National Archives)

overestimated the strength of his existing Panzer divisions, many of which had been in continuous action for several weeks and had not had their losses made good.

The bulk of von Kluge's strike force had to be gathered from those armoured divisions already at his disposal. All of his Panzer divisions were either employed in the line or worn out and in need of refitting. Hitler had authorised the release of a new corps and two new divisions from elsewhere in France to join in the attack. The 9th Panzer Division was ordered to Normandy from Avignon in the south and 708th Infantry Division was redeploying from Royan; both would be under the command of LXXXI Corps when it arrived from Rouen. Neither division made it to Mortain, however, both being halted further south by Patton's forces. Von Kluge agreed with Eberbach that the armoured divisions of II SS-Panzer Corps could not be spared as all three were in action with the British to the east of Vire and to withdraw them would almost certainly mean the collapse of the whole front. He had no choice but to husband his forces and assemble units from along the front, at the same time under pressure from the Führer who wanted to see his plans and what forces he intended to use, and to know the intended start date.

By 5 August, the C-in-C (West) had decided the attack would be made by XLVII Panzer Corps led by Gen der Panzertruppen Hans von Funck. It would contain 1st and 2nd SS-Panzer Divisions, 2nd and 116th Panzer Divisions, together with groups from 17th SS-Panzergrenadier and 275th Infantry Divisions. LXXXI Corps would also take part. In total, von Funck had about 120 tanks and 32 assault guns and tank destroyers with which to attempt to break through to the sea.

The Mortain counterattack, Operation *Lüttich,* was launched on 7 August, but without the element of surprise, Bradley having been forewarned of the impending strike by 'Ultra' intercepts and aerial reconnaissance. To counter the German move, 30th Infantry Division was placed in Mortain and told to expect the enemy attack. When it began, 2nd SS-Panzer Division 'Das Reich' immediately ran into trouble, proving unable to evict the American 30th Division from the important height of Hill 317 south of Mortain. Some enemy penetration was made further to the north, but within 24 hours Bradley had assembled seven divisions under the command of US VII Corps to seal off the enemy operation. The German counterattack soon petered out and was pushed back to its start line.[7]

## Operation *Totalise*

The gains made by Operations *Bluecoat* and *Cobra* in the western sector led the enemy to transfer some of his armour from south of Caen. First to redeploy was 21st Panzer Division at the end of July, followed by 1st and 9th SS-Panzer Divisions during the first days of August. On 4 August, after his forces had engaged these armoured divisions in the west, Montgomery ordered the Canadians to renew their advance with a heavy attack towards Falaise.

The Commander of Canadian II Corps, LtGen Simmonds, had been planning the move for some time, as the enemy in front of him posed some special problems. After Operation *Goodwood* had been called off with just modest gains on 20 July, the enemy had spent a good deal of time improving his defences and fortifying a string of villages lining the route south to Falaise. His main line of defence linked La Hogue, Tilly la Campagne and May sur Orne across the Caen–Falaise highway. All of these villages had seen heavy fighting over the previous weeks, but all attempts to capture them had failed. The enemy resolutely defended these localities and had even constructed a second defensive line eight kilometres further back between St Sylvain and Bretteville sur Laise. Central to the defence of these lines was a powerful screen of anti-tank weapons, many of which were the dual purpose anti-aircraft/anti-tank 88mm guns of III Flak Corps, which was still deployed east of the River Orne. The open countryside south of Caen allowed these weapons to dominate all Allied movement and made the armour particularly

---

7 See Campaign 88 *Operation Cobra 1944* for a detailed analysis of Operation *Lüttich*.

vulnerable during an attack. Artillery fire and long-range mortars were also well suited to counter any attacks across the wide, flat farmland devoid of hedges or cover.

The direction and objectives of the proposed Canadian operation could not be disguised. The enemy knew that the attack was coming and he also knew from which direction. To meet such a frontal attack he was prepared to employ his usual tactics of holding the line with lesser infantry whilst keeping his elite armoured forces dispersed in the rear, held back to counter any Allied penetration wherever it might occur.

Obergruppenführer Josef 'Sepp' Dietrich, Commander I SS-Panzer Corps, held the line in front of Canadian II Corps between May sur Orne and La Hogue with 89th Infantry Division. 272nd Division held the line east from La Hogue to the junction with LXXXVI Corps, facing the Canadians and the flank of British I Corps. Dietrich's armoured reserve was the now tired 12th SS-Panzer Division 'Hitlerjugend', which had been in almost continual action since 7 June. Reinforcement in the shape of 85th Infantry Division was on its way from 15th Army but was not due to arrive in the area until 9 August. Dietrich also had around 21 Tiger tanks of 101st Heavy Tank Battalion in support.

LtGen Guy Simmonds and his planners had given considerable thought to the problem of breaking through the strong German line. Other attacks in the area, most notably Operation *Goodwood* and the renewed attacks down the Caen–Falaise highway the previous week, had all been stalled by heavy anti-tank fire and well-placed enemy positions. Once his tanks and infantry had left the start line and moved out onto the flat, open countryside, they were extremely vulnerable to accurate German fire. Simmonds also knew that a successful penetration of this outer crust would bring his forces almost immediately into the armoured second line of defence. He decided that he would need to approach these problems in a new way and employ many unorthodox methods to overcome the enemy's obvious advantages.

The attack, Operation *Totalise*, would begin at nightfall and continue through the hours of darkness. The initial penetration would be made

The Caen–Falaise highway on the first day of Operation *Totalise*. The picture is taken near the start line of the battle and the sky on the right is thick with the smoke of the many fires caused by air attacks and artillery beyond the village of Roquancourt. (Imperial War Museum, HU52361)

by infantry and armour together. The assaulting infantry would be carried forward in American-built half-tracks and armoured vehicles specially modified to carry troops, thus giving them speed of advance and some protection from enemy fire. Some would ride in carriers that had been converted from Priest self-propelled gun chassis. These armoured vehicles had landed with the Canadian field regiments on D-Day but had by then been superseded and replaced by Sexton self-propelled guns and towed 25-pdr field guns. The 105mm weapon had been removed and the chassis modified to carry a section of infantrymen. The mobile infantry and tanks would press through the main German defence line on to their objectives in front of the second line, leaving the marching infantry following behind them to deal with any pockets of the enemy who had been bypassed during the attack.

The advance would on this occasion not be preceded by the usual heavy artillery barrage to force the enemy into cover and blast a hole for the attacking infantry. Montgomery had once again been given the air support of RAF Bomber Command and US Eighth Air Force. Lancaster and Halifax heavy bombers would attack the enemy's defences both in front of the Canadians and in the villages either side of the Caen–Falaise road on the flanks of the proposed penetration, starting their raid 30 minutes before the infantry moved off. The next day, American Flying Fortress and Liberator bombers would bombard the German second line of defence eight kilometres to the rear of their first line just before the advancing Canadians reached it. Artillery fire would of course be available to support particular attacks and the fighter bombers of RAF 2nd Tactical Air Force would be on hand to strike identified targets during daylight hours.

For Operation *Totalise*, LtGen Simmonds would use his Canadian 2nd and 3rd Infantry Divisions supported by the tanks of the Canadian 4th Armoured Division and the Canadian 2nd Armoured Brigade. His corps would be reinforced by the newly arrived Polish 1st Armoured Division and the loan of two units from British I Corps, 51st Highland Division and 33rd Armoured Brigade. The infantry of 51st Division and the tanks of 33rd Armoured Brigade would lead off the attack to the east of the Caen–Falaise highway, attacking La Hogue, Cremesnil and St Aignan. At the same time, Canadian 2nd Division, supported by Canadian 2nd Armoured Brigade, would strike to the west of the road

against Roquancourt and Caillouet. The next day, sometime after midday, Canadian 4th Armoured Division and Polish 1st Armoured Division would be introduced into the battle. They would pass through the infantry and attack the second line of defences immediately after the USAAF had released a second load of bombs on the enemy positions around the villages of Bretteville sur Laize, Hautmesnil and St Sylvain. On the left flank of Canadian II Corps, British I Corps would act to prevent any counterattacks from the Vimont area. As the operation developed, I Corps would take over the eastern side of the penetration.

Operation *Totalise* began at 23.00hrs on 7 August with over 1,000 aircraft of RAF Bomber Command unleashing a devastating array of high explosives on the flanks of the Canadian attack. The area between La Hogue and Mare de Magne in the east and Fontenay le Marmion and May sur Orne in the west was enveloped in clouds of dust and flame thrown up by the bursting bombs. This aerial bombardment continued unabated for the next hour, shattering the German 89th Division and having a similar effect on the morale of the survivors, leaving the unit incapable of interfering with the Canadian attack. By midnight dust and smoke had so obscured the targets that the bombers were ordered to break off the raid and return to their bases. Just over 60 per cent of the bombers had by then delivered their payload, with the loss of ten aircraft to enemy flak.

At 23.30hrs the two infantry divisions, shadowed by the tanks of their accompanying armoured brigades, opened their attack. Each assaulting division led off with two groups of two columns. Each column contained four long lines of closely packed armoured vehicles guided by navigating tanks and preceded by flail tanks, with the gun tanks screening the infantry carriers. Streams of coloured tracer shells fired by Bofors guns in the rear marked their route through the darkness, and clouds of dust thrown up by the aerial bombardment. Artificial moonlight was provided by searchlights bouncing their beams off the low clouds. Early progress was good despite some loss of direction and many collisions amongst the tightly packed groups. The 3,462 tons of bombs dropped by the RAF had shattered the enemy in front of them and most of the

Sherman tanks of Canadian 4th Armoured Division moving up to join in the second phase of Operation *Totalise*. (Ken Bell/National Archives of Canada, PA-140822)

Polish armour from Polish Divisional Reconnaissance Regiment lined up in columns on the flat plain south of Caen ready for their introduction into the second phase of Operation *Totalise*. The regiment was equipped with Cromwells and these can be seen in the column on the right. On the left is a commander's Sherman tank showing three aerials, with a line of Stuart light tanks behind. (Imperial War Museum, B8835)

early objectives on the high ground astride the main road five kilometres behind the German front line had been taken by first light. Behind the leading waves the infantry advancing on foot continued to mop up the enemy in the villages bypassed during the assault.

On the left, 51st Division supported by 33rd Armoured Brigade had taken La Hogue, Tilly la Campagne and Secqueville la Campagne. On the right, the battered ruins of Rocquancourt, Fontenay le Marmion and May sur Orne had likewise fallen. In some places fighting had been heavy, especially for those battalions involved in mopping up. During the morning Simmonds' two armoured divisions, neither of which had previously seen action, began moving up ready to join in the second phase of the operation. MajGen G. Kitching's Canadian 4th Armoured Division and MajGen S. Maczek's Polish 1st Armoured Division had only arrived in Normandy a short time before and this was to be their first battle. Their task was to assault and break through the enemy's second line and to push on and seize the high ground eight kilometres short of Falaise. The third phase of the operation would see these forces encircling the town while the infantry attacked its centre.

Just prior to the second bombing raid, Standartenführer Kurt Meyer, Commander 12th SS-Panzer Division 'Hitlerjugend', had come forward to the area of Cintheaux to direct his counterattack against the Canadian penetration. Through his field glasses he could see the vast numbers of Polish and Canadian tanks massing for a fresh assault and knew that such an attack would be preceded by an artillery barrage and perhaps a fresh bombing raid. The presence of marker aircraft over the battlefield confirmed his suspicion. He therefore arranged for some of his troops and armour to retreat from the second line before the bombardment, and to prepare to launch an immediate counterattack against the Allies as soon as the barrage ended.

Up until around midday on 8 August things had gone well for Simmonds. The German front line had been broken and his forces were poised to attack the second line. Everyone now awaited the arrival of the

# OPERATIONS *TOTALISE* AND *TRACTABLE*

Canadian breakout battles fought along the Caen—Falaise road against I SS Panzer Corps.

Note: Gridlines are shown at intervals of 2 km/1.24 mile

**ROESLER** 8

**DANNHAUSER** 271st

FONTENAY LE MA

BRETTEVILLE SUR L

12

11

POINT 195

POTIGNY

15

SOUMONT-ST
QUENTIN

18

J

POINT 159

L 19

K

21

14

FALAISE

RIVER ANTE

MORTEAUX-COULI

**ALLIED UNITS**

- **A** 154th Brigade, 51st Highland Division
- **B** Canadian 4th Brigade, Canadian 2nd Division
- **C** Canadian 6th Brigade, Canadian 2nd Division
- **D** Canadian 2nd Armoured Brigade
- **E** British 33rd Armoured Brigade
- **F** Canadian 4th Armoured Division
- **G** Polish 1st Armoured Division
- **H** Canadian 28th Armoured Regiment (British Columbia Regiment), Canadian 4th Armoured Division
- **I** Canadian 4th Armoured Brigade
- **J** Canadian 10th Armoured Regiment (Fort Gary Horse)
- **K** 22nd Armoured Regiment (Canadian Grenadier Guards) Canadian 4th Armoured Division
- **L** Regina Rifles Regiment, Canadian 7th Brigade, Canadian 3rd Division

**GERMAN UNITS**

- **1** 1055th Grenadier Regiment, 89th Infantry Division
- **2** 1056th Grenadier Regiment, 89th Infantry Division
- **3** 101st Heavy Tank Battalion
- **4** Battle Group Waldmuller (from 25th SS Panzergrenadier Regiment) and II Battalion 12th SS Panzer Regiment both from 12th SS Panzer Division
- **5** HQ Defence battalions of 12th SS Panzer Division and 1 SS Panzer Corps
- **6** Battle Group Krause (26th SS Panzer Grenadier Regiment) 12th SS Panzer Division

**MEYER** 12th SS

 EVENTS

**1** **Operation *Totalise* begins at 2300 hours on 7 August when areas around the villages of May sur Orne, Fontenay, St Aignan and Secqueville in front of the Canadian II Corps are bombed by over 1,000 aircraft so as to isolate the flanks of the attack.**

**2** 2330 HOURS, 7 AUGUST: **154th Brigade of 51st Highland Division, supported by 33rd Armoured Brigade, advance from the start line and attack the villages of Tilly la Campagne, Garcelles and St Aignan held by German 1055th Grenadier Regiment.**

**3** 2330 HOURS, 7 AUGUST: **Canadian 4th Brigade of Canadian 2nd Infantry Division, supported by Canadian 2nd Armoured Brigade, start their attack against German 1056th Grenadier Regiment in the villages of Verrières and Rocquancourt.**

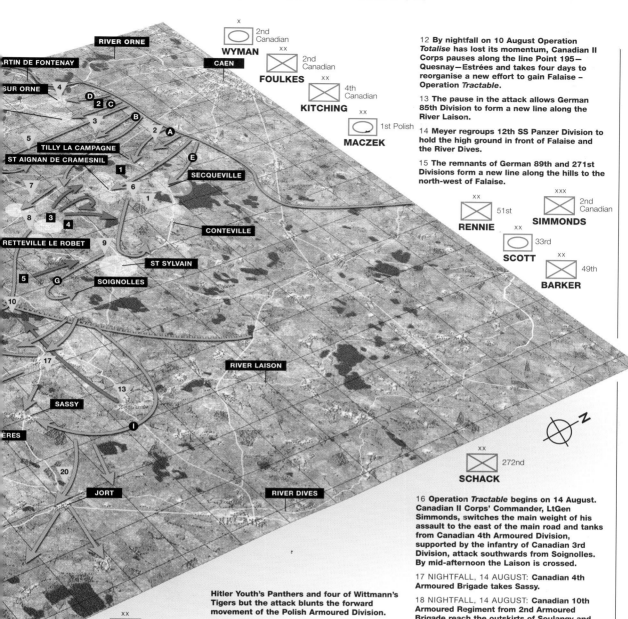

**RIVER ORNE**

x
2nd Canadian
**WYMAN**

xx
2nd Canadian
**FOULKES**

**CAEN**

xx
4th Canadian
**KITCHING**

xx
1st Polish
**MACZEK**

RTIN DE FONTENAY

SUR ORNE

4

D
2 C
3
B
2 A

5

**TILLY LA CAMPAGNE**
**ST AIGNAN DE CRAMESNIL**

1
E

7

6
**SECQUEVILLE**

1

8  3
4

**CONTEVILLE**

RETTEVILLE LE ROBET

9

**ST SYLVAIN**

5
G
**SOIGNOLLES**

10

17

**RIVER LAISON**

13

**SASSY**

ÈRES

I

20

**JORT**

**RIVER DIVES**

xx
85th
**CHILL**

xx
51st
**RENNIE**

xxx
2nd Canadian
**SIMMONDS**

xx
33rd
**SCOTT**

xx
49th
**BARKER**

xx
272nd
**SCHACK**

N

12 **By nightfall on 10 August Operation** *Totalise* **has lost its momentum, Canadian II Corps pauses along the line Point 195— Quesnay—Estrées and takes four days to reorganise a new effort to gain Falaise – Operation** *Tractable.*

13 **The pause in the attack allows German 85th Division to form a new line along the River Laison.**

14 **Meyer regroups 12th SS Panzer Division to hold the high ground in front of Falaise and the River Dives.**

15 **The remnants of German 89th and 271st Divisions form a new line along the hills to the north-west of Falaise.**

16 **Operation** *Tractable* **begins on 14 August. Canadian II Corps' Commander, LtGen Simmonds, switches the main weight of his assault to the east of the main road and tanks from Canadian 4th Armoured Division, supported by the infantry of Canadian 3rd Division, attack southwards from Soignolles. By mid-afternoon the Laison is crossed.**

17 NIGHTFALL, 14 AUGUST: **Canadian 4th Armoured Brigade takes Sassy.**

18 NIGHTFALL, 14 AUGUST: **Canadian 10th Armoured Regiment from 2nd Armoured Brigade reach the outskirts of Soulangy and take the village the next day to seize the Caen—Falaise road behind the German-held Potigny.**

19 15 AUGUST: **a fierce delaying action is fought around Point 159 by Battle Group Krause from 12th SS Panzer Division and Canadian 22nd Armoured Regiment is repulsed. Further attacks by the Regina Rifles Regiment take the hill and open the way into Falaise.**

20 15 AUGUST: **Polish 1st Armoured Division attack south-eastwards and seize a crossing over the important River Dives, leaving the way to Trun open. This puts Allied troops on the eastern banks of the Dives in a position to close the rapidly forming 'pocket' of German forces between Falaise and Argentan.**

21 16 AUGUST: **Canadian infantry and tanks reach Falaise and enter the town against fanatical resistance from the Hitler Youth of 12th SS Panzer Division who fight a famous last stand amongst its ruins.**

4 **Following behind 4th Brigade, Canadian 6th Brigade attack the flanking villages of May sur Orne and Fontenay le Marmion.**

5 MORNING OF 8 AUGUST: **Canadian attacks on the eastern side of Caen—Falaise road, now supported by tanks from Canadian 4th Armoured Division, are stopped by enemy resistance in area of Bretteville and Cintheaux.**

6 **Polish 1st Armoured Division comes forward to resume armoured advance south eastwards from St Aignan.**

7 **Commander 12th SS Panzer Division, Kurt 'Panzer' Meyer, comes forward to Cintheaux and organises a counter attack against the Polish Armoured Division. He sends an infantry/armoured counter attack against St Aignan. Heavy fighting destroys many of the**

Hitler Youth's Panthers and four of Wittmann's Tigers but the attack blunts the forward movement of the Polish Armoured Division.

8 **Heavy bombers from 8th USAAF bomb the villages in front of the advancing Canadian II Corps but inaccurate bombing causes significant numbers of casualties amongst the Polish and Canadian troops.**

9 AFTERNOON, 8 AUGUST: **renewed attacks by Polish 1st Armoured Division against St Sylvain are met by counter attacks by tanks and infantry of 12th SS Panzer Division and I SS Panzer Corps.**

10 NIGHT OF 8/9 AUGUST: **tanks and infantry from Canadian 28th Armoured Regiment advance on Point 140 in error and are immediately counter attacked and destroyed by the remaining Tiger tanks of 101st Heavy Tank Battalion together with infantry from German 85th Division and Panthers from 12th SS Panzer Regiment. The Canadians lose 47 tanks.**

11 **Canadian attacks against Point 195 to the west of Caen—Falaise road are initially repulsed but succeed by the end of 10 August.**

heavy bombers of the USAAF. At around 12.30hrs the American aircraft began their attack. It was a fine day with clear skies as the first of the 678 bombers of US Eighth Air Force approached from the west through fairly heavy flak and began bombing St Sylvain and Bretteville sur Laize, their targets picked out by coloured markers fired by the artillery. Once the dust and smoke from the raid started to drift across the battlefield, their aim drifted a little wide of the targets. Although the 492 aircraft who actually released their bombs mainly dropped their loads on the enemy, considerable areas of the Canadian rear were hit. Over 300 casualties were suffered by Canadian, Polish and British troops from the deluge of high-explosive and fragmentation bombs that fell amongst them, including the commander of Canadian 3rd Division, MajGen Rod Keller. Ten American bombers were brought down by flak during the raid to the ironic cheers of the watching Canadians.

Once the bombers had left the area, the Canadian and Polish attack resumed. At the same time Meyer brought forward his Panzers: two battlegroups of Panthers and PzKpfw IVs supported by the Tigers of 101st SS-Heavy Tank Battalion and a few assault guns. These small groups of tanks together with large numbers of 88mm guns made skilful use of what cover was available and wrought havoc amongst the advancing Allied armour. To the west of the main road the Canadians took Bretteville sur Laize, but to the east of the highway the Poles were held up around St Aignan de Cramesnil. One of the actions fought by 101st SS-Heavy Tank Battalion brought to an end the career of Hauptsturmführer Michael Wittmann, hero of the action at Villers Bocage against British 7th Armoured Division in June. Wittmann now led his company of Tiger tanks from the area to the east of Cintheaux against the troops attacking St Aignan de Cramesnil, but his attack was beaten off by anti-tank guns and Sherman Fireflies sporting the long 17-pdr gun. Wittmann's tank was destroyed in the encounter and its commander and all of its crew killed. Fierce fighting continued during the afternoon of 8 August, but Canadian II Corps were unable to make much further progress southwards, gradually losing the impetus gained by the carpet-bombing raid.

During the night, the enemy made a partial withdrawal into a third line of defence three kilometres further back running along the high ground to the north of Potigny and the steeply wooded valley of the River Laison to the east of the Caen–Falaise highway. Work had begun on these positions a week earlier, and Dietrich now ordered as much of his infantry and as many guns as possible back into this line, including the shattered remnants of 89th Division. The Germans then deployed a screen of 88mm guns along this line, backed up with mobile groups of tanks and Panzergrenadiers. The I SS–Panzer Corps commander also had the luxury of reinforcements to help stiffen this line, as the infantry of 85th Division began to arrive from Fifteenth Army.

At first light the next day, 9 August, the Canadian attack resumed, but made little progress. The enemy guns and tanks hidden in woods and small copses hit the advancing tanks from all sides. The Polish armour went beyond St Sylvain, but failed to penetrate the villages below the new German defence line. The enemy's 88s dominated the battlefield engaging any tank that showed itself in the open. Above the battlefield fighter-bombers swooped down on targets identified by ground observers, but the enemy guns and tanks were well hidden. During that day and the next, the village of Bretteville le Rabet was occupied by Canadian 4th Armoured Division, as was the important height of Hill 195 to the west of the road, albeit after several failed attempts. Further advance southwards, however, faltered, trying to take the heavily defended Quesnay Wood. It seemed that every thrust by the Canadians was countered by Meyer's troops. The commander of 'Hitlerjugend' was making very skilful use of his limited resources.

Simmonds' armour had failed to break into the new German line, except in one isolated case. A penetration did cause the enemy some concern when tanks of the 28th Armoured Regiment (British Columbia

Tanks of Polish 10th Armoured Cavalry Brigade, 1st Armoured Division, wait in line before being called forward to support the attack by 51st Highland Division on the left flank of Operation *Totalise*. (Imperial War Museum, B8826)

The ground over which German tank ace Hauptsturmführer Michael Wittmann advanced towards St Aignan with his group of Tiger Is on 8 August. The German tanks were fired on by the 17-pdr gun of a Sherman Firefly from 3 Troop, A Squadron, of the Northamptonshire Yeomanry. Three German tanks were knocked out, including that of the company commander. Wittmann and all of his crew were killed. (Ken Ford)

Regiment) and two companies of infantry from the Algonquin Regiment set out to take Hill 195 west of the highway, but got hopelessly lost. At 07.55hrs on 9 August they reported that they were on Hill 195, but were in fact on Hill 140, over 6,000 metres from their objective and to the east of the main road. They had established themselves almost on top of the new German line, which was still under construction. 'Panzer' Meyer's reaction to this penetration was swift; the Canadian outpost was attacked from three sides throughout the day by tanks from Obersturmbannführer Max Wünsche's 12th SS-Panzer Regiment, Panzergrenadiers of I Battalion, 25th SS-Panzergrenadier Regiment and by the infantry of 85th Division. Tanks circled the exposed Canadians and inflicted dreadful carnage, whilst the whole area was bombarded by artillery fire. Eventually it became clear that the exposed position astride Point 140 could not be held and those Canadians that had survived the onslaught withdrew. The British Columbia Regiment lost 47 tanks in the action and suffered 112 casualties, of whom 40 were killed, including their commanding officer, LtCol D.G. Worthington. The Algonquin Regiment suffered similar losses with 45 men dead out of a casualty list of 128.

By 10 August, everyone connected with the battle was becoming frustrated. Montgomery's patience with Crerar's army was wearing thin. Two massive aerial bombardments and overwhelming numbers of tanks and infantry had failed to break through the German line barring the road to Falaise. Both of the armoured divisions hammering at the enemy were new to battle and were not performing well. It was later revealed that German tank strength facing Canadian II Corps had been reduced to just 35 by the end of 10 August: 15 Panzer IVs, 5 Panthers and 15 Tigers. Countering these, LtGen Simmonds had around 700 tanks on call, together with an infantry superiority of around three to one. Despite this he could not bludgeon his way past Dietrich's depleted forces. He had advanced ten kilometres (6.2 miles) through heavily defended country, but was still 20 kilometres (12.4 miles) short of Falaise. It became clear to all concerned that a new approach was

needed to re-energise the attacks. Simmonds called off Operation *Totalise*, pulled back his armour and held the line with the two Canadian infantry divisions while he formulated a new plan. In the meantime, the Germans continued to burrow their way underground along the heights beyond the River Laison.

# THE ENCIRCLEMENT

On 8 August, while the American First, British Second, and Canadian First Armies were fighting bitterly for each new yard of Normandy soil, General Patton and his forces were making sweeping gains in the south. US Third Army had passed through the bottleneck at Avranches and was advancing against very light opposition. German Seventh Army had all of its strength in the line facing northwards and westwards with little in the rear to oppose these mobile thrusts. To the west, US VIII Corps had troops closing around the Brittany fortresses of St Malo, Brest, Lorient and St Nazaire. In the south US XX Corps was almost on the River Loire and to the south-east US XV Corps was at Le Mans, sending Hausser's HQ scurrying away to the east.

At this time Montgomery and Eisenhower were still working to the plan to push back the Germans towards the Seine. British and Canadian forces were to pivot at Falaise and swing eastwards to the river, forcing the retreating enemy through the Orléans–Paris gap, while Patton's army swung round their southern flank to cut off their retreat. At the appropriate moment, two Allied airborne divisions would then be dropped into the gap at Chartres to seal the enemy's escape route. On 8 August it occurred to Bradley that the German counterattack at Mortain could not achieve its objectives and that by attacking westwards whilst Patton was attacking eastwards, von Kluge was committing strategic suicide. German forces were in great danger of being completely outflanked. If Patton's forces now turned north towards Alençon, at the same time as the

Canadian First Army advanced southwards through Falaise, then German Seventh and Fifth Panzer Armies would be completely encircled when the two Allied armies linked up. Bradley conferred with Eisenhower and suggested that one of Patton's corps should turn north. Eisenhower readily agreed and reassured Bradley that if the Germans actually succeeded in cutting off Patton's advancing troops he would arrange to have 2,000 tons of supplies delivered per day by air. Eisenhower then put the plan to Montgomery. He too saw the logic in such a move and approved the manoeuvre. He then urged Crerar to concentrate every effort on his Canadian offensive towards Falaise, launched the night before, and then to push on for Argentan. Monty was confident that the Canadians would beat the Americans to the town. In turn Bradley ordered Patton to send XV Corps northwards from Le Mans through Alençon to meet the Canadians.

At the same time that Eisenhower was contemplating the capture of German Seventh and Fifth Panzer Armies, von Kluge was signalling to his masters at OKW that the attack towards Avranches was no longer feasible. Allied aircraft were making all movement very difficult and the resistance put up by the Americans was too strong for his depleted forces to overcome. He also pointed out that the concentration of Panzer forces at the western end of the front was aiding the British in their advance in the east. Generalfeldmarschall von Kluge's pleas were rejected by Hitler and he issued new orders. The attack was now to be taken over by Eberbach, who would relinquish Fifth Panzer Army to 'Sepp' Dietrich. General der Panzertruppen Eberbach's new command became 'Panzer Group Eberbach' and was subordinated to Hausser's Seventh Army. It would now thrust south-westwards from Domfront and then turn north-westwards towards the sea. The order was complete madness. Hitler was still focussed on attacking westwards and ignoring the danger that was looming over his forces from the south. Those German commanders closer to the front could see the enormity of the danger, but there was little they could do in the face of the Führer's wilful blindness. Hitler could not have played more into the hands of the Allies if he had tried.

Patton's unit commanders responded to their new orders with alacrity. MajGen Haislip quickly consolidated at Le Mans and XV Corps was ready to advance northwards on 10 August. Patton gave Haislip an additional armoured division for the move in the shape of Général de Division Jacques Phillipe Leclerc's 2nd Armoured Division (2ème Division Blindée). It now became the first French division to engage in fighting the Germans on French soil and the local civilians burst into a patriotic furore wherever it appeared.

The XV Corps attacked with 5th Armored Division (MajGen Oliver) in the lead followed by 79th Infantry Division (MajGen Wyche) heading for Sées and French 2nd Armored Division followed by MajGen McLain's 90th Infantry Division towards Alençon. Both towns were reached and taken by 12 August, despite some German opposition from 708th, 9th Panzer divisions and the heavily battered 352nd Division. Thirty-six tanks were lost during the drive, but the greatest source of

Whilst Patton's US Third Army grabbed all the headlines dashing across Brittany and sweeping down to the Loire, Hodges' US First Army was still slogging away through thick countryside driving a resilient German Seventh Army back into the pocket that was forming around Hausser's command. (US National Archives)

frustration for Haislip's corps was the large traffic jams in the rear as the four divisions forced their way forwards. The Americans were now just 20 kilometres south of Argentan; the Canadians had been stopped dead 35 kilometres to the north of the town. This 55-kilometre corridor was still wide enough to give the enemy an escape route.

When Eberbach arrived to take over his newly named Panzer group he was appalled by the spectre that greeted him. His armoured forces had been decimated by air attack, the supporting infantry were exhausted, much of their equipment was broken and ammunition and fuel stocks were low. He told von Kluge that he could not possibly launch a new attack towards the sea before 20 August, until he had reorganised his command. Hitler insisted that it be mounted the next day, 11 August. However, by the evening of 10 August the change of direction of US XV Corps had become apparent and the seriousness of the situation was only too clear to von Kluge and Hausser. The Commander-in-Chief (West) and Commander of Seventh Army both agreed that further efforts towards Avranches had no prospect of success and signalled to OKW that the attacks should be broken off to permit a shifting of forces to counter the moves by Patton's corps. The whole of the next day was taken up in trying to persuade Hitler to change his mind and agree to this move. Eventually the Führer relented and approved a minor withdrawal around Mortain, but insisted that the attack towards the sea be resumed immediately US XV Corps had been halted.

With the breakout of Patton's Third Army causing all sorts of problems for von Kluge, Bradley continued to engage the Panzer forces facing his First Army, in an effort to tie them down and prevent them from moving south. General Hodges was ordered to return to the offensive now that the German attack through Mortain had been blunted. On 12 August US V and XIX Corps were once again on the move, with their advance swinging around from the south to the east, pushing back the extended left flank of German Seventh Army. Further south, MajGen Collins pivoted his US VII

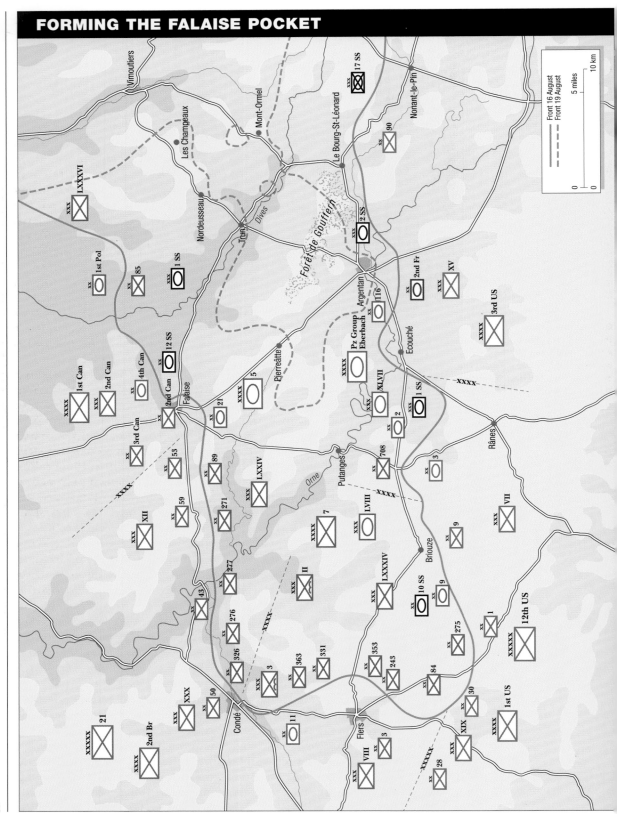

Gen Montgomery is introduced to the senior officers of Polish 1st Armoured Division by its commander MajGen Maczek, the day before the start of Operation *Totalise*. (Imperial War Museum)

Corps north-eastwards from Mayenne ... gap between his corps and US XV Corps ... more pressure to bear on the bulge that ... created by the gradual encirclement of ... forces.

In the north, Dempsey's British Second Army continued its drive south and east. On 12 August, XII Corps had crossed the Orne north of Thury Harcourt and cleared the Forest of Cinglais to come up onto Canadian II Corps' right flank. LtGen Ritchie's corps then captured Thury Harcourt the next day and was soon advancing south-eastwards along the road that led from the town towards Falaise. Horrocks and XXX Corps had continued the move towards Condé sur Noireau and VIII Corps was closing on Tinchebray and Estry, but both of these corps continued to meet almost fanatical resistance. Von Kluge's forces were now in action on three fronts, with the 'pocket' shrinking under the inexorable weight of Allied arms. The enemy remained capable of putting up determined resistance wherever he was pressed too hard, however, as the Canadians found to their cost when they resumed the advance on Falaise.

By 13 August it was realised by everyone that the Germans were in a catastrophic position. The Allies saw a very real possibility of surrounding von Kluge's forces and annihilating or capturing his two armies. The enemy's only remaining escape route to the east was through a 50-kilometre gap that was shrinking by the hour. The entire German effort should by then have been concentrated on fighting their way clear of the trap, but to their Supreme Commander retreat was anathema. The closing of the gap now became an important Allied priority, but not an overriding one. The enormity of the opportunity within their grasp was not fully appreciated. Bradley and Montgomery now both made decisions that later came back to haunt them and to puzzle future historians.

At 23.30hrs on 12 August, Haislip informed Patton that his 5th Armored had achieved its objective and was on the verge of securing Argentan. Haislip now asked for new orders as he had no mission beyond the town. He asked if he could continue northwards into British 21st Army Group territory until he met the Canadians. Patton told him to wait until he had consulted with Bradley. In a magnificent piece of Anglophobia, Patton told Bradley that Haislip had elements in Argentan and asked 'Should he now continue and drive the British into the sea for another Dunkirk?' Bradley replied in the negative, ordering Patton not to go beyond Argentan. He feared that interference with established boundaries might cause confusion. Patton tried to persuade him, but Bradley stood firm and even got Ike's confirmation of the decision. Neither of the two top US commanders put the question to Montgomery, nor asked for the inter-Allied boundary to be moved northwards. Patton was furious; Haislip's continuing his advance made military sense and would precipitate a German collapse. In the meantime Haislip had, with Patton's blessing, allowed his men to push slowly around and past Argentan and these troops were not recalled

until the afternoon of 13 August. By then they had met stiffening resistance; the enemy had switched 116th Panzer Division and elements of 1st and 2nd SS-Panzer Divisions from Panzer Group Eberbach to counter US XV Corps' advance. Patton's requested swift advance on Falaise might have met a bloody repulse had his flanks been hit by these elite formations. Incredibly, the enemy were still more intent on stopping the Allies' advance than in organising an escape from the looming encirclement.

On 13 August Montgomery remained hopeful that the Canadians could make a swift drive to Argentan through Falaise. Although he was disappointed with the performance of Crerar's army he made no move to reinforce it, or to switch the main weight of his advance down the vital Caen–Falaise–Argentan road to link up with Patton and seal the gap. All now depended on the big new Canadian set-piece attack on Falaise, Operation *Tractable*.

## OPERATION *TRACTABLE*

LtGen Simmonds' new plan was to make the primary thrust to the east of the main road. To confuse the enemy, several spoiling moves were made to the west of the road on the 12 and 13 August, striking across the River Laize at Bretteville and moving south to come abreast of Point 195 and British 53rd Division who had crossed the Orne north of Thury Harcourt. This put Canadian 2nd Division in a position to threaten Dietrich's left flank. Unfortunately, these deceptions were undermined by the German discovery of some notes on the body of a dead Canadian officer that he had made at a corps' briefing. These showed that Simmonds intended to throw the main weight of his attack to the east of the Caen–Falaise highway. This allowed 12th SS-Panzer Division 'Hitlerjugend' to make effective, last-minute preparations to receive the blow.

Once again the attack would be concentrated on a narrow front with the assaulting infantry carried in armoured carriers. Two columns, each

Sherman tanks of Polish 1st Armoured Division waiting to enter the second phase of Operation *Totalise* on 8 August. (Imperial War Museum, B8830)

led by an armoured brigade and followed by two infantry brigades would rush the enemy. On the left was Canadian 4th Armoured Division, with Canadian 3rd Infantry Division on the right, supported by Canadian 2nd Armoured Brigade. They would cross the River Laison between Montboint and Maizières, wheel south and make for the high ground north of Falaise, most especially Hill 159 that overlooked the town. There would be no prior artillery barrage, with the tanks and infantry relying on the smokescreen and surprise to outwit the German defences during the initial advance. Massive air support was once again available to Simmonds, this time by the RAF and RCAF, with medium bombers attacking the area of the German defences along the Laison and heavy bombers striking the enemy on the right flank of the advance by laying a carpet of high explosive across the main road both above and below Potigny. As the advance rolled out, Polish 1st Armoured Division would then cross the Laison further downstream and swing southwards alongside Canadian 4th Armoured Division. Once the enemy had been cleared from the ground to the north of Falaise, Canadian 2nd Infantry Division would capture the town. The armoured divisions would then continue round its eastern side, cross the River Dives and make for Argentan with all speed to meet up with Patton's troops. To support the entire left wing of the attack, British I Corps would advance with its 49th Division towards Mézidon and the 51st Division towards St Pierre sur Dives.

Operation *Tractable* began at 11.45hrs on 14 August and kicked off with a massive smokescreen to blind the enemy, rather than the darkness relied on in Operation *Totalise*. The new offensive got off to an optimistic start with both columns reaching and crossing the Laison in good time. Once across and onto the wooded high ground beyond, they were met by heavy enemy fire. The Canadians then began to take heavy losses in tanks and infantry. Fighting was confused and direction was often lost in the smoke and dust thrown up by the armoured vehicles. Later in the afternoon more infantry joined the leading troops and the

advance regained some momentum, but German resistance was still ferocious. At 14.00hrs, the heavy bombing programme began along the main highway to the west of the attacking troops, concentrating on enemy positions in front of Canadian 2nd Division. Once again the bombing was somewhat wayward and disruptive. Most of the bombs found their correct targets, but 77 of the 800 bombers that the RAF and RCAF put into the air dropped their bombs on friendly troops. Over 400 casualties resulted, including 65 dead.

The good start made by Canadian II Corps was marred by a slowing down of progress as the Canadians moved further into the heavily defended ground. Simmonds urged his troops on, demanding that Falaise be taken as soon as possible. Canadian 2nd Division advanced directly towards the town from the north-west and Canadian 3rd Infantry swung round to the west aiming for Hill 159 finding it very hard going. The Germans contested every metre of ground. The next day progress was even slower, with gains dwindling and the momentum flagging. Hill 159 was eventually reached and taken by 3rd Division on 16 August, while on the same day 2nd Division fought its way to the outskirts of Falaise, but it took two more days for the division to completely clear out the Panzergrenadiers of 12th SS-Panzer Division from its ruins.

On 15 August, 1st Polish Division crossed the River Dives to the east of Falaise, followed by Canadian 4th Division a little further upstream the next day. This put the two armoured divisions well east of the Falaise–Argentan road and on a direct route to Argentan, but on 16 August changes had been made to the rendezvous point. Argentan was no longer the goal; the meeting place and the closing of the gap had been switched to Chambois.

## Patton Moves East

In the south enemy resistance to the American moves around Argentan was increasing in ferocity. Stuck at Argentan on the 13 August by Bradley's directive, Patton decided to continue his move eastwards towards the

Seine, implementing the original plan to create a wider encirclement of German forces in front of the river. First, he left two of his divisions – French 2nd Armoured and US 90th Divisions – in the Argentan area and then reinforced them by moving MajGen McBride's 80th Division up from XX Corps. On 15 August he cut loose the rest of Haislip's corps together with its HQ. His 5th Armored and 79th Infantry Divisions now set out towards Dreux and the Seine. The three divisions left behind were taken over by a scratch corps HQ under MajGen Gerow, whose own US V Corps had been pinched out of the fighting in the north. Gerow made tentative moves along the Argentan front and switched some of his armour to the north-east, but everywhere he found German resistance had been stiffened by the arrival of Panzer Group Eberbach.

With little in front of them, Haislip's depleted corps made it to the Seine on 17 August, arriving in the area near Mantes Gassicourt. Two days later, 79th Division slipped a battalion across the great river over a damaged weir and formed a small bridgehead. This was immediately enlarged by the remainder of the division and the news signalled to Patton. His men had breached the final German defence line in France. Also ready to move east on 14 August were US XII, XIX and XX Corps, heading for Orléans, Chartres – liberated on 16 and 18 August respectively – and the great prize of Paris. The need for an airborne operation to help the advance and cut off the enemy was now pointless. The Germans in Normandy were being completely outflanked.

Back around Argentan new moves were afoot. It was clear by 15 August that the Canadians were making such slow progress taking Falaise that they would not reach Argentan and close the pocket for some time. It was therefore agreed with Montgomery that the gap would now be closed along the River Dives, with the meeting place of the two Allied armies being shifted to Chambois. Argentan would now be taken by the Americans and Gerow would continue his northwards advance to the north-east to link up with Simmonds' corps.

The bridge at St Lambert sur Dives over which a great mass of German armour and transport escaped during the final days of the pocket. (Ken Ford)

American infantry involved in street fighting on the outskirts of Brest. Although the port was reached by the vanguard of the US 6th Armored Division on 6 August, the city did not fall to the Americans until 16 September. The German soldiers defending the fortress belonged to the 2nd Parachute Division and the 343rd Infantry Division and they fought tenaciously to prevent the great port falling to the Allies. By the time the demolished dock installations were in American hands, the front had moved on to Belgium and Holland, too far away for Brest to be of any real use to the Allies. (US National Archives)

While these moves were being implemented, the bulk of von Kluge's two armies were still facing north and west. Panzer Group Eberbach had swung southwards on 13 August to face Patton and was heavily engaged denying Argentan to the Americans. The balance of German formations still struggled just to hold the line. Although many of the top commanders in the field could see from their situation maps that a great crisis was developing, there was still no concerted move to escape the trap whose jaws were closing around them, although some German units were moving east as they were pinched out of the shortening front line.

The truly desperate nature of their plight became apparent during 15 August. On that day the entire German front continued to be forced back by Allied pressure and cracks began to appear everywhere. Hitler and the OKW received further dispiriting news with new Allied landings in the south of France along the Riviera coast. German forces in France now had to contend with a threat from a new direction just as the Normandy front began to collapse. Further cohesion was lost in Normandy when von Kluge went missing for the entire day. He had been caught up in a fighter-bomber attack whilst moving between headquarters, lost both of his signals trucks and spent the day in a ditch completely out of touch with any of his forces. When news of his disappearance reached Hitler he became suspicious. Von Kluge had been loosely linked with the assassination attempt on Hitler's life on 20 July and Hitler now doubted the loyalty of his field marshal. He believed, wrongly, that von Kluge was meeting with the Allies to arrange a surrender. When the Commander-in-Chief (West) turned up the next day the situation facing his two armies was beyond redemption. He signalled OKW with a report that insisted that all troops in the western salient be evacuated immediately through the gap that still existed north of Argentan. He even went so far as to issue the order to prepare for a general withdrawal, although stopped short of

actually implementing the evacuation. Hitler finally conc
agreed that von Kluge's forces should withdraw to a new line
River Dives. He also relieved GFM von Kluge of his com
ordered him to return to Berlin. The field marshal complie
directive, but fearful of his fate he committed suicide en route.

Von Kluge was replaced by GFM Walther Model, one of Hitler's
favourite field marshals and a hero of the Eastern Front. His arrival was
too late to have any substantive effect on the situation. All energy was
now directed towards getting as many men and as much equipment out
of the pocket as possible. First priority was to extricate II SS-Panzer
Corps from the encirclement and withdraw it to the area of Vimoutiers.
Here it was to be reorganised into a strike force that would be used to
keep the mouth of the encirclement open. Eberbach was now told to
organise and lead this battlegroup.

# DESTRUCTION OF AN ARMY

On 16 August, when Canadian II Corps broke through Fifth Panzer
Army's front at Falaise and British Second Army reached the area to the
west of the town, the enemy knew that the battle of Normandy had
reached crisis point. German Seventh Army was implementing a gradual
withdrawal back across the Orne towards the River Dives and Panzer
Group Eberbach was doggedly defending the southern flank of the bulge.
The German commanders all knew that they were in great danger of
being encircled. The prospects looked grim, but as yet there was no panic.
A general withdrawal had been ordered and would be implemented in
the usual efficient German manner. Rigid timetables and objectives were
issued, the use of specific roads allocated, crossing places controlled and
phased objectives planned. Whilst a gap remained between Falaise and
Argentan, there was a possibility that the two armies could escape from
the encirclement and fall back behind the River Dives.

Allied airpower wrecked most of these well-laid plans, however.
Throughout the hours of daylight the skies over Normandy swarmed
with Allied fighters, fighter-bombers and medium bombers flying
countless missions to harass any and all enemy movement. With the very
real danger of encirclement, the German withdrawal to the east had to
take place round the clock and, for almost the first time since D-Day,
large German troop movements took place in daylight. The Falaise
pocket became a killing ground; British and American fighter-bombers
pounded any visible German units with rockets and cannon fire.

Nevertheless, four days after Montgomery had agreed with the
Americans that he would close the pocket at Argentan with all speed, his
troops were still 20 kilometres from the town and 25 kilometres from the
new Anglo-American rendezvous at Chambois. The Americans were less
than impressed. Montgomery, aware that a great opportunity was
slipping away, urged Gen Crerar to seal off the pocket more quickly. He
ordered that Crerar's armoured divisions push all-out for Trun and
Chambois on the River Dives. Dempsey's Second Army was still fighting
doggedly through the confines of the close countryside surrounding the
Orne, pushing the left wing of Fifth Panzer Army and the right wing of

British Cromwell tanks meet up with American infantry near Argentan as the two sides push German Seventh Army deeper into the trap that was closing around it. (Imperial War Museum, 9534)

Seventh Army steadily backwards. Hodges' US First Army was doing the same at the western and southern extremities of the pocket, closely pursuing Hausser's men as they fell back. Both armies were using all their military might to exert pressure on the pocket, but the coup de grâce could only be delivered once the German escape route had been cut and the pocket sealed. Everything depended on Crerar's First Canadian Army linking up with the Americans at Chambois and closing the trap.

Canadian 4th and Polish 1st Armoured Divisions were now directed towards the important road junction of Trun in the Dives valley, seven kilometres north-west of Chambois. The Canadian division advanced on the right, fighting its way slowly forward against elements of several formations from Fifth Panzer Army. It reached the area to the east of Trun on 18 August and then assisted Canadian 3rd Division in taking the town. To its left, Polish 1st Armoured Division had been told to swing east of Trun to get round to Chambois. It also had to fight numerous individual skirmishes with Panzer units fleeing the pocket and was unfortunate to encounter II SS-Panzer Corps (2nd and 9th SS-Panzer Divisions) struggling eastwards. The SS troops were trying to reach their rallying point at Vimoutiers, to prepare to hold open the escape route from the pocket open. As a result of this encounter the Poles were forced further to the east than intended, swinging south to Chambois over Mont Ormel, the long spur of high ground at Coudehard overlooking the Dives valley. They were now advancing across the enemy escape route and were embroiled in almost constant actions with German units attempting to flee from the encirclement. MajGen Maczek realised that this high ground was the key to sealing the pocket and established his armoured division on the escarpment on 18 August. He was determined to hold the heights, which he called the 'Mace' because its shape reminded him of a medieval club, and began shelling the Germans fleeing across and around his positions. Maczek then organised a battlegroup to descend into the valley and seize Chambois.

A Polish Sherman tank preserved at the visitor centre on Mont Ormel as a memorial to the 1st Polish Armoured Division who fought such a brave action on the surrounding slopes. (Ken Ford)

By this time BrigGen Raymond McLain's US 90th Division and elements of the French 2nd Armoured Division were fighting their way towards the meeting place at Chambois. The closer they got to the town, the heavier the enemy resistance became. Chambois and Trun had become the shoulders of the gap and it was imperative for the Germans that the roads through them remained open. When, on 18 August, Trun fell to the Canadians, the enemy lost one of its vital crossing points over the River Dives. Only two bridges now remained in German hands, one at St Lambert sur Dives, four kilometres south-east of Trun, the other three kilometres further along the valley at Chambois. Between the two, at Moissy, was a solitary ford that led onto a small country lane. On 18 August, these three routes were the only practicable remaining means of escape for German Seventh and Fifth Panzer Armies.

The pocket had now become a burning cauldron ringed almost completely by superior troops and constantly pounded by artillery and aircraft. The forces inside the pocket were beginning to lose all cohesion. Days of constant attacks had wreaked terrible havoc. Whole divisions and corps increasingly existed in name only; units were been broken up by Allied penetrations and further dispersed by the constant bombing and shelling. Most transport vehicles had been destroyed or abandoned and the German communications net within the pocket had broken down almost completely. Supplies of all descriptions were running low, particularly ammunition, fuel and food, and resupply was out of the

A view of the Dives valley from the commanding heights of Mont Ormel. The lane from St Lambert sur Dives runs across the middle of the picture. All the Germans who escaped during the final few days of the pocket had to cross the valley floor and then climb up and over Mont Ormel in the face of Polish guns deployed on these slopes. (Ken Ford)

Columns of enemy transport heading eastwards to escape from the Allied encirclement. These long lines of vehicles became constant targets for Allied aircraft. Just below the centre left of the picture, the transport is negotiating its way around a large crater. The fleeing armour did not have to stick to the roads and tank tracks can be clearly seen cutting across the fields. (Imperial War Museum, CL839)

question. Support units were ordered out of the encirclement and were joined by a mass of individual fugitives who had lost their units. It began to appear as if the entire German Army in Normandy was disintegrating into headlong flight. For the Germans, the battle for Normandy now came down to a struggle for individual survival. Nonetheless, the massed evacuation of the pocket still had to be controlled; it was not yet every man for himself. It was imperative that some units stood and fought to buy time for others to disengage and withdraw.

On 17 August the German commanders felt the pressure had eased marginally. The Canadian penetrations east of Falaise seemed to have been sealed off and the Americans in the south were not pushing as hard. Hausser and Eberbach believed that that they could carry out their withdrawal across the Orne and Dives within two or three nights. Indeed, that night plans for units to disengage and withdraw proceeded successfully. Although the situation remained critical, still there was no panic.

The withdrawal of Seventh Army across the River Orne was achieved under the most difficult of circumstances. Almost all of its units were fiercely engaged with the Allies. In spite of steep river banks, very few bridges, and the attentions of enemy artillery and fighter-bombers, the divisions were pulling back in remarkably good order. The army commander later explained how this was done: 'It was achieved through the loosening up and wide dispersal of our formations, the distribution of the movement over two nights and the strict regulation of the traffic over the bridges.' His forces used bridge commanders at each crossing place, with widely separated points of departure for the retreat. Good telephone communications between the commanders were essential to ensure that a unit only began to retreat when the signal was given that the road ahead was clear. They also maintained a ruthless policy of removing all broken down vehicles along the routes.

On 18 August, both Hausser and Eberbach were ordered to meet with GFM Model at his HQ outside the pocket at Fontaine l'Abbé to report the situation. Hausser was reluctant to leave his post and sent his Chief of Staff, Oberst Freiherr von Gersdorff in his place. By then Trun had been lost so the two men came out of the pocket via the bridge at St Lambert sur Dives. Based on their reports, Model ordered both armies to withdraw across the Dives during the following two nights and to regroup on a new river line based on the Touques. Simultaneously, II SS-Panzer Corps would attack from the Vimoutiers region towards Trun to keep open the gap. Von Gersdorff then left to return to Hausser in the pocket on foot and Eberbach went on to Vimoutiers to command II SS-Panzer Corps' counterattack.

That same day the Canadians began moving along the Dives valley towards Chambois to link up with the Poles and the Americans. A combat group from 4th Armoured Division made up of about 175 men, and including tanks, self-propelled anti-tank guns and infantry of the Argyll and Sutherland Highlanders of Canada, gained a foothold in St Lambert and established themselves on a height overlooking the village. The force was commanded by Major D.V. Currie of the Canadian 29th Armoured Reconnaissance Regiment (South Alberta Regiment). The Canadians were now positioned astride one of the main escape routes from the pocket and encountered streams of German infantry, guns and tanks all intent on making their escape. From their vantage point,

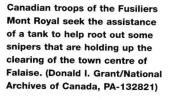

**Canadian troops of the Fusiliers Mont Royal seek the assistance of a tank to help root out some snipers that are holding up the clearing of the town centre of Falaise. (Donald I. Grant/National Archives of Canada, PA-132821)**

# SEALING THE POCKET

On 19 August Canadian, Polish and American forces combined to close the gap. The two main escape routes were the foot bridge at St Lambert and the ford at Moissy. On 20 and 21 August the remnants of the German Seventh and Fifth Panzer Armies made last attempts to get across the river before the pocket was finally sealed.

Note: Gridlines are shown at intervals of 2 km/1.24 mile

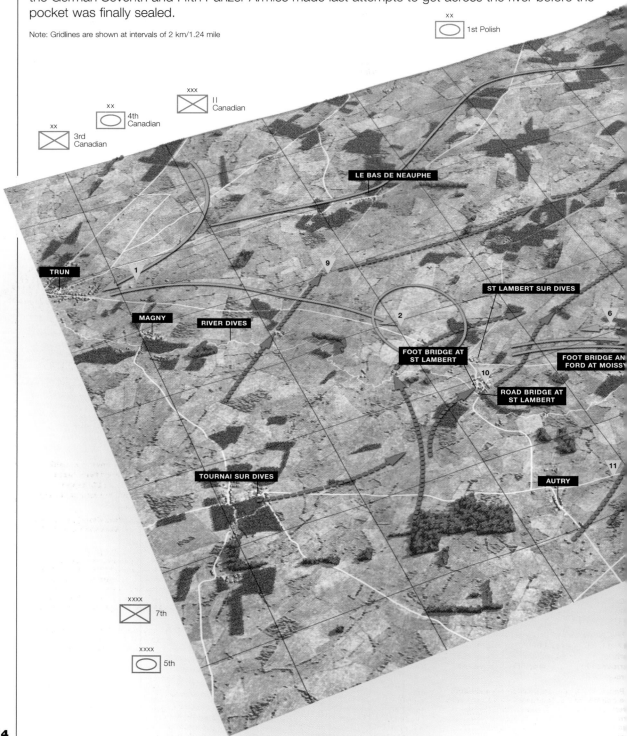

1st Polish

4th Canadian

II Canadian

3rd Canadian

LE BAS DE NEAUPHE

TRUN

1

9

ST LAMBERT SUR DIVES

6

MAGNY

RIVER DIVES

2

FOOT BRIDGE AT ST LAMBERT

FOOT BRIDGE AND FORD AT MOISSY

10

ROAD BRIDGE AT ST LAMBERT

TOURNAI SUR DIVES

11

AUTRY

7th

5th

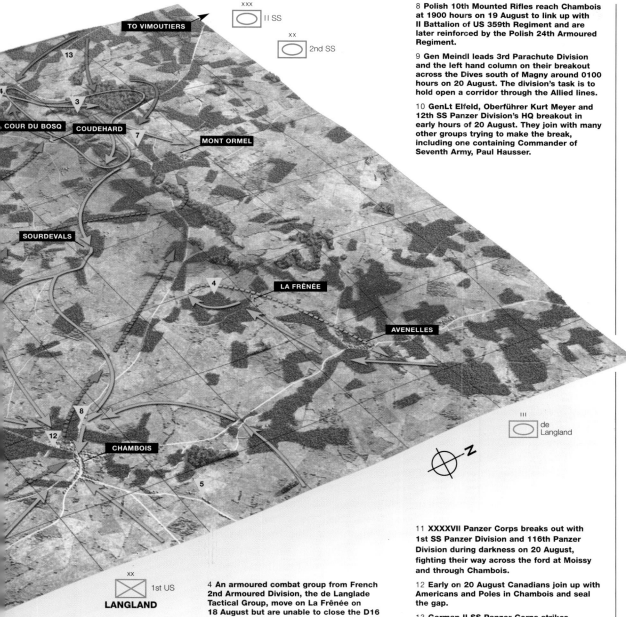

**8** Polish 10th Mounted Rifles reach Chambois at 1900 hours on 19 August to link up with II Battalion of US 359th Regiment and are later reinforced by the Polish 24th Armoured Regiment.

**9** Gen Meindl leads 3rd Parachute Division and the left hand column on their breakout across the Dives south of Magny around 0100 hours on 20 August. The division's task is to hold open a corridor through the Allied lines.

**10** GenLt Elfeld, Oberführer Kurt Meyer and 12th SS Panzer Division's HQ breakout in early hours of 20 August. They join with many other groups trying to make the break, including one containing Commander of Seventh Army, Paul Hausser.

**11** XXXXVII Panzer Corps breaks out with 1st SS Panzer Division and 116th Panzer Division during darkness on 20 August, fighting their way across the ford at Moissy and through Chambois.

**12** Early on 20 August Canadians join up with Americans and Poles in Chambois and seal the gap.

**13** German II SS Panzer Corps strikes southwards from Vimoutiers in order to join up with those elements of Seventh and Fifth Panzer Armies trying to clear the pocket. Furious fighting takes place with the Poles around Point 262. German 2nd SS Panzer Division reopens the Chambois—Vimoutiers road.

**14** Gen Meindl attacks with a battle group of 3rd Parachute Division and a few tanks to clear the Poles from road from La Cour-du-Bosq to Boisjos to reopen the escape route eastwards allowing some German tanks, guns and transport to escape from the cauldron. Polish 1st Armoured Division is completely surrounded and cut off.

**15** On 21 August Polish 1st Armoured Division is relieved by elements of Canadian 4th Armoured Division and the last escape route is closed.

## EVENTS

Canadian 4th Armoured Division arrive to ᵗhe east of Trun on 18 August and finally ᶜapture the town later that day.

Maj Currie's small battle group seize Hill ᴵ17 and northern end of St Lambert sur Dives ᵉarly on 19 August and are soon attacked and ˢurrounded by the enemy fleeing eastwards ᵗhrough the village.

Polish 1st Armoured Division advance onto ᵗhe heights above Coudehard on 18 August to ᵒverlook the escape route of German 7th ᴬrmy. Attempts that day to move south ᵃgainst Chambois fail against heavy ʳesistance.

**4** An armoured combat group from French 2nd Armoured Division, the de Langlade Tactical Group, move on La Frênée on 18 August but are unable to close the D16 road from Chambois to Vimoutiers. Against American orders, the group retires back behind the River Dives.

**5** US 358th and 359th Infantry Regiments of US 90th Division arrive on the southern and eastern outskirts of Chambois on 18 August and then move into the town the next day to meet with the Poles advancing down from Mont Ormel.

**6** Canadian 4th Armoured Division try to join up with the Americans and Poles in Chambois early on 19 August but are turned back by the enemy who are streaming through the rapidly closing gap in the pocket.

**7** Polish 1st Armoured Division attack southwards from Coudehard and Point 262 crossing the Chambois—Vimoutiers road on 19 August in an attempt to join up with the Americans around Chambois.

Currie and his men brought down well-aimed artillery on the enemy as they made repeated attempts to force the Canadians off the hill. Any of the enemy who crossed the bridge heading east had to run this gauntlet of concentrated fire.

On 19 August, Currie and his men fought their way into St Lambert and tried to capture the bridge. The flood of enemy troops pouring through St Lambert proved too great for the small force to deal with and Currie's men withdrew back into a defensive perimeter atop the hill. There they remained for two more days harassing the withdrawal and capturing hundreds of the enemy. Thousands of German troops streamed through St Lambert, almost all of whom were preoccupied with escape to the east rather than trying to winkle out a stubborn pocket of enemy troops supported by a prodigious amount of artillery. For his gallant feat of arms at St Lambert sur Dives against overwhelming numbers of the enemy, Maj Currie was awarded the Victoria Cross, the first Canadian VC to be won during the campaign in North-West Europe.

The roads running out of the valley of the Dives from St Lambert and the ford at Moissy both led up over the heights of Coudehard known to the locals as Mont Ormel. Commanding these heights was Maczek's 1st Polish Armoured Division. Once the enemy had squeezed through the bottlenecks around the River Dives and escaped into the countryside, he was then faced with the Poles lining the high ground in front of him across which he must find a route to escape the Allied net. Streams of Germans made their way up and over Mont Ormel, passing either side of the guns of the Polish division. Yet again these unfortunates were subjected to a deluge of shelling all the way, and their misery compounded by Allied air activity overhead and by long-range artillery fire from Canadian guns to the north. Thousands of Germans were killed and wounded in the leafy lanes and pastures below Mont Ormel.

In addition to inflicting as much damage as possible on the withdrawing German forces, MajGen Maczek also turned his attention to seizing Chambois and closing the gap once and for all. From his positions on Mont Ormel he was already overlooking the roads to the east and bringing fire down on the German escape routes, but he had not achieved Canadian First Army's prime objective of linking up with the Americans. He dispatched a battlegroup down from Mont Ormel to fight its way into the town against the flood of escaping Germans. On 19 August, tanks and infantry of the Polish 10th Armoured Cavalry Brigade advanced westwards between the road leaving the ford at Moissy and the Chambois–Vimoutiers road that led up across Mont Ormel. The 10th Polish Dragoons swung round behind a slight promontory, Hill 113, and attacked the northern edge of the town, while the Polish 24th Lancers and the Polish 10th Mounted Rifle Regiment passed to the south of the hill and also hit the town from the north. Fighting was fierce as the Poles encountered groups of the enemy determined to fight their way through to the east. The fugitives continued pushing through Chambois to make their escape and the German force ordered to defend the town resisted desperately. Their orders were to hold the southern shoulder of the escape route and keep it open at all costs. The German position deteriorated further as US 90th Infantry Division also attacked Chambois from the south and a combat command of the French 2nd Armoured Division, the de Langlade Group, tried to cut the road to the east. After fighting of almost unbelievable ferocity, the town finally fell to the Poles and the Americans. The two Allied armies had, at last, joined up, in theory closing the pocket. But with Allied forces still painfully thin on the ground and the Germans desperate to break out of the trap, the seal was not yet hermetic.

Many of the senior German commanders were still inside the pocket at this point. Seventh Army Chief of Staff, von Gersdorff, returned to the pocket late on 18 August with news of GFM Model's orders to withdraw all forces back behind the Dives the following night. Hausser's HQ had just one day to organise this withdrawal. On 18 August the pocket was still open and hopes were high that most of the troops could be extricated.

It became clear to all the next day, however, that an orderly withdrawal from the ever-shrinking pocket was impossible. The gap had been closed, but local intelligence suggested that it had not been completely sealed.

A wounded German soldier receives medical attention from a Canadian medic during the fighting for Trun. (Donald I. Grant/National Archives of Canada, PA-152377)

The loss of Chambois and the presence of Canadians along the Trun–Chambois road meant those German troops remaining within the pocket would undoubtedly have to fight their way out. Virtually all of their transport was gone and that which remained continued to attract the attention of roaming Allied aircraft. Almost all of the units still in the pocket were reduced to fragmented battlegroups and combat commands led by junior officers and NCOs. Almost the entire area of the Falaise pocket was by now within range of Allied artillery. Seventh Army HQ was shelled and moved to Villedieu les Bailleul near St Lambert, where it was shelled again. There seemed to be no escape from the bombardment. The point at which it would become every man for himself was rapidly approaching.

During 19 August, Hausser's staff worked on the plan for the breakout. The II SS-

## A COUNTER ATTACK BY 2ND SS PANZER DIVISION 'DAS REICH' TRIES TO EVICT POLISH 1ST ARMOURED DIVISION FROM MONT ORMEL DURING THE EARLY MORNING OF 20 AUGUST 1944 (Pages 78-79)

MajGen Maczek had brought his Polish 1st Armoured Division up onto the heights above Coudehard when he swung his advance eastwards around Trun on his way to capture Chambois (1) to meet up with the Americans. In doing so he placed his division across the route of those Germans trying to escape the pocket being formed in front of the River Dives (2). Once on this high ground of Mont Ormel, the Polish Division soon became engaged by the enemy streaming up and over its slopes towards Vimoutiers. Almost immediately, Maczek's division was cut off from Canadian First Army and surrounded. The Poles had no option but to fight on alone, eventually being supplied with ammunition and food from the air. In the valley of the River Dives below, individual troops and tracked vehicles from German Seventh Army and Fifth Panzer Army try to make their way across fields to reach the routes that lead out of the area. Artillery fire (3) from the Americans to the south and Canadians to the north is exploding across the valley floor as these two Allied armies close around the enemy forces trapped in the pocket. Along the road that leads up from Chambois towards Vimoutiers (4) a burning German column (5) has been hit by rocket-firing Typhoon aircraft and blocks the road. On 20 August, Eberbach's II SS Corps attacked the Poles from the direction of Vimoutiers to hold open the route eastwards for one last desperate attempt to escape by the fleeing Germans inside the pocket. Polish 1st Armoured Division was hit by tanks and panzergrenadiers of the 2nd SS Panzer Regiment, from 2nd SS Panzer Division 'Das Reich'. The force of the assault brought the SS troops right amongst Maczek's positions. The enemy tank (6) is a Panzer V Panther which had been in action since June; the wavy texture to the surface of the Panther's 'Zimmerit' anti-magnetic paste, designed to prevent the attachment of magnetic charges, is showing signs of wear (7). The 'Das Reich' Division arrived in Normandy from Montauban in southern France after a notorious march during which it committed the infamous atrocities and massacres of French civilians in Tulle and Oradour sur Glane. A Polish light tank M5 Stuart (8) from a reconnaissance platoon has been knocked out by the German tank and is burning furiously. It has been almost blown apart by the Panther's main weapon; the crew would not have had time to bail out. A Sherman tank from Polish 1st Armoured Regiment (9) of the division has reversed into a hedge backed by trees in an effort to escape the German tank and is trying to bring its gun to bear on the Panther. Although almost overrun by the 2nd SS Panzer Division, the Polish troops hung on tenaciously to their high ground, refusing to give way. In the afternoon the attack was broken off by the SS troops and Maczek was able to send a battlegroup down to Chambois to close the gap with the Americans.

The scene in one of the lanes in the Dives valley that led eastwards from the pocket. British troops examine the mass of debris left after the battle. (Imperial War Museum, CL909)

Panzer Corps would attack from Vimoutiers towards Trun with 9th SS-Panzer Division while 2nd SS-Panzer Division cleared the Polish Armoured Division from Mont Ormel. The Germans would take advantage of these diversions to break as many units as possible out of the trap. All available men would be subordinate to and directed by a corps headquarters. Two main groups would make the breakout. GenLt von Choltitz and his LXXXIV Corps HQ would command the northern group, which would cross the River Dives on both sides of Trun. To the south, II Parachute Corps HQ, led by General der Fallschirmjäger Meindl, would effect an escape on both sides of St Lambert sur Dives. They would leave behind rearguards who would follow later and who would stage a prolonged defence on the Dives. General der Infanterie Straube and LXXIV Corps HQ would command the west of the pocket as it shrank and would follow behind the other corps as part of the rearguard. Panzer Group Eberbach, still holding back the Americans, would make its escape around Chambois. Start time for the operation was nightfall.

The German plan was undermined even before it began. Late afternoon brought the realisation that the area around Trun was now impenetrable and that Chambois was in the hands of the Allies. All the escaping groups would now have to force their way out across the Dives either side of St Lambert. What vehicles there were would have to cross at either the bridge at St Lambert or the ford at Moissy. Those escaping on foot were left to cross the Dives where they could.

As night fell the drama began to unfold. Guided by compass through a night sky illuminated by the flashes of gun fire and the impact of high

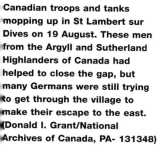

Canadian troops and tanks mopping up in St Lambert sur Dives on 19 August. These men from the Argyll and Sutherland Highlanders of Canada had helped to close the gap, but many Germans were still trying to get through the village to make their escape to the east. (Donald I. Grant/National Archives of Canada, PA- 131348)

**ESCAPING TROOPS FROM GERMAN SEVENTH ARMY AND FIFTH PANZER ARMIES ARE CAUGHT BY ROCKET-FIRING TYPHOON AIRCRAFT IN A NARROW LANE EAST OF THE RIVER DIVES ON 20 AUGUST 1944** (PAGES 82-83)

By 19 August, the inexorable advance of four Allied armies had squeezed Gen F.M. Model's forces in Normandy into a pocket which was continuing to shrink by the hour. The only means of escape from what had become a burning cauldron was across the River Dives between Trun and Chambois. That night a final withdrawal was organised during which the bulk of those inside the trap were to flee eastwards towards Vimoutiers. Two main crossing places over the Dives were open: one a bridge at St Lambert, the other a ford at Moissy. From each of these two crossing places a narrow lane led over the valley floor across a landscape of small fields and high hedges, up to the heights above Coudehard at Mont Ormel. These were the only routes passable for transport. Individuals of all ranks, from private to general, had to take to the fields on foot. The operation got underway as soon as darkness fell, but the scale of the exodus and the numbers of vehicles converging on the crossing places inevitably led to congestion. Further confusion was added by the continual fire of Allied artillery which probed the night, seeking assembly points and crossing places. By morning, the stream of fleeing enemy was still in full spate. The dark which had screened the flight now slipped away and the long lines of helpless Germans were lit up by an unpitying August sunshine. Canadian and American artillery fire pounded the lanes whilst waves of rocket-firing aircraft (1) swept down to blast the enemy. It was a killing ground. The lane quickly became blocked by damaged vehicles and tanks, causing all progress to halt while the debris was pushed aside. Maddened horses harnessed to smashed wagons ran rampant until silenced by painful deaths. (2) Armoured tanks were blown completely apart by the explosive power of rockets. (3) Bodies of dead men and animals were crushed underfoot as the tanks and lorries all tried to charge their way through the mêlée. No one knows the true number of Germans killed in the onslaught; the total most likely ran into thousands. Gen Eisenhower later commented that it was possible to walk for miles stepping on nothing but dead and decaying flesh. Local civilians speak of a great black cloud hovering over the lanes during the days that followed the closing of the pocket, as swarms of flies and maggots devoured the bodies of the dead.

RIGHT **The fortified manor farm of Boisjois on the edge of Mont Ormel, surrounded for three days by the enemy. The picture is taken from the road along which escaping German armour and transport flowed up over the hill and out of the encirclement. (Ken Ford)**

ABOVE **The road of death that ran from St Lambert sur Dives up to Mont Ormel along which so much destruction took place during the German escape from the pocket. (Ken Ford)**

explosives, various groups snaked their way down to the River Dives. Most were on foot, escaping as ad hoc groups guided by higher command. The Commander-in-Chief Seventh Army, Paul Hausser, marched out on foot, machine-pistol slung over his shoulder, with some of the staff of II Parachute Corps HQ. More than half of all staff officers of his army had been wounded and were being transported out on vehicles of Panzer Group Eberbach via the ford at Moissy. Hausser got down to the river near St Lambert and crossed the Dives via a narrow footbridge under artillery and anti-tank fire. He picked his way through the village and set out along the lane that led up to the heights above Coudehard, where Maczek's Poles were blocking the road, but was forced to take shelter in an orchard when day broke. Other senior commanders joined the foot soldiers moving across fields, along hedges and then across the river, braving the machine-gun fire and shells that raked the entire Dives valley. Kurt 'Panzer' Meyer, commander of the 12th SS-Panzer Division, led a group of his men across the river below St Lambert. In the darkness he lost contact with his men and continued alone, skirting a number of Canadian positions before eventually reuniting with the few members of the group that survived the breakout.

Throughout the daylight hours of 20 August the withdrawal continued along routes that were often cut by Canadian tanks moving along the Trun–Chambois road. Battlegroups from individual German divisions had to fight their way out across the Dives and up the lanes. In the fields between the Dives and Mont Ormel, senior officers gathered what infantry they could and those armoured vehicles to hand and made an assault against Maczek's Poles blocking the road over the escarpment. Generals Hausser and Meindl personally organised a battlegroup of two tanks and a party of men to attack along the single road over the escarpment to make their escape. In the process, Hausser had his jaw smashed by shellfire. Time and again groups of men forced a way through the Polish line only for it to close behind them once again.

The attack by II SS-Panzer Corps, which should have been co-ordinated to coincide with the breakout during the night, was delayed and did not begin until 04.00hrs on 20 August. The armoured corps sent 9th SS-Panzer

Division towards Trun to push back the Canadians at the same time as 2nd SS-Panzer Division struck the Polish Armoured Division from the rear. Maczek's men were concentrating all their fire on the German forces moving from the west when the tanks of 2nd SS-Panzer Division hit them from the east. Thousands of Germans swarmed past on either side of their positions, but every time the Poles tried to block the escape route it was blasted open again by determined enemy combat groups. Entirely surrounded, Maczek's division was forced to fight the battle unaided.

Throughout 20 August fighting raged across the top of Mont Ormel. The SS troops were determined to drive the Poles off the top of the escarpment and clear the way for their escaping comrades but Polish resistance was dogged and they threw back any enemy that penetrated their lines and several positions atop the ridge changed hands a number of times. Supplies were dropped to the besieged Polish armoured division from the air when ammunition began to run short.

The fortified manor at Boisjois was the highest point on Mont Ormel and it overlooked the winding road over the hill along which the Germans were escaping. It also sat across the road from the east, down which 2nd SS-Panzer Division was attacking. Throughout the night of 19/20 August the roads passing Boisjois teemed with German traffic, all of it trying desperately to escape to the east. The fortified position around the manor was too strong for the Germans to attack, so their columns trudged wearily by as the Poles poured fire into them. Around dawn Boisjois was attacked by several Panther tanks and Panzergrenadiers from 2nd SS-Panzer Division. The Poles replied with anti-tank and tank fire forcing the enemy back. This was the first of a series of assaults that swept against the Polish positions again and again during the day. The Poles held firm, throwing back every attack, but suffered dreadful casualties in the process.

By late afternoon, II SS-Panzer Corps' attack was called off. It had not succeeded in clearing the Polish division from Mont Ormel, nor in driving through to Trun, but its intervention had diverted Allied attention sufficiently to allow great numbers of Germans to escape over the heights of Mont Ormel. The next day Canadian 4th Armoured fought its way through to relieve Maczek's isolated division, and more and more Canadian and American troops pushed along the Dives valley to finally and decisively close the Falaise pocket.

# AFTERMATH

The final closing of the gap between Trun and Chambois on 21 August allowed the Allies to take stock of the situation. They had undoubtedly won a great victory, of that there was no doubt, but many of the enemy troops along with some of his armour and guns had escaped towards the Seine. Some of this equipment was overtaken and captured or destroyed during the subsequent retreat before reaching the Seine, and more was wrecked during the crossing. A good deal was isolated by the wider encirclement effected by US forces, who had reached the Seine before the gap was closed and had driven down the left bank of the river towards Rouen mopping up the enemy as they went. This wider encirclement did not allow the Germans to establish any kind of defensive line along the Seine and the enemy had no choice but to continue falling back, closely pursued by the Allies right across France almost to the German border.

The destruction of Seventh Army and the greater part of Fifth Panzer Army had resulted in the deaths of thousands of German soldiers. No accurate official figure can be given, but estimates put the number between 10,000 and 15,000. Many more were wounded and thousands of others captured; around 50,000 of the enemy became prisoners of war. Virtually all of the enemy's equipment, guns and tanks were destroyed or lost. German figures show that somewhere between 30,000 and 50,000 men escaped from the pocket.

German troops captured by B Company, Argyll and Sutherland Highlanders of Canada, in St Lambert sur Dives on 19 August, just as the escape route was being closed. Many German commanders, including Hausser, passed across this road here on the night before the picture was taken to make their escape. Maj David Currie, VC, is the officer in the left foreground holding the pistol. (Donald I. Grant/National Archives of Canada, PA-116586)

British Second Army and US First Army deserved great credit for their part in the victory and for their continual pressure that had played a significant role in the formation of the pocket in the first place. Although the trap had been snapped shut by Canadian 1st Army and US Third Army, Hodges' and Dempsey's forces had fought a most difficult battle of attrition, grinding down a determined and well-entrenched enemy, and suffering great numbers of casualties in the process. Success south of Falaise led to the rapid pursuit across France and into Belgium and saved the Allied forces from having to fight a series of bitter battles to breach a succession of German defence lines as they advanced.

Well before the pocket was closed, the Supreme Commander, Gen Eisenhower, was looking towards the next phase of the campaign. The landings in southern France, Operation *Dragoon*, had opened up a new front and one of his prime considerations was linking Gen Jacob Devers' 6th Army Group (US Seventh and French First Armies) with that of Bradley's 12th Army Group in the north. Between them was the uncommitted German First Army, but that was already falling back rapidly towards the German border and the western environs of Paris. The whole of central France was being evacuated voluntarily, although German Nineteenth Army which had been guarding the Mediterranean coast was fighting a spirited rearguard up the Rhône valley as it retired north in the face of Devers' advance. Bradley now instructed Patton to send a corps south-eastwards to meet with French First Army near Dijon linking the two fronts. The remainder of US First and Third Armies would advance on a broad front to the Seine and beyond.

In the north Montgomery's 21st Army Group now had to wheel around to the left, facing east for its own advance to the River Seine. General Crerar's Canadian First Army would move across northern France with its left flank on the Channel coast, aiming for the Seine north of Rouen. Dempsey's army would advance on its right flank

between the Canadians and the Americans and make its crossings over the river between Rouen and Mantes Gassicourt. The area upstream including Paris was to be the responsibility of the Americans.

Already on its way eastwards was Crocker's British I Corps. Not involved in closing the pocket, by 17 August it was fanning out beyond St Pierre sur Dives with an almost clear run to the Seine. In the northern sector along the coast, MajGen Gale's 6th Airborne Division and the two supporting commando brigades (1st and 4th Special Service Brigades) were at last preparing to leave the confines of the airborne bridgehead they had occupied since D-Day. On 17 August they tentatively inched their way past an almost deserted Troarn and the next day fanned out to began their sweep along the Channel coast towards the Seine.

No significant German forces remained to face the Allies after the Normandy debacle. Rapid progress was made everywhere. Paris fell on 25 August and the British made their first crossing of the Seine that day at Vernon. Patton crossed the River Meuse on 31 August and was at Metz on the Moselle the next day. Brussels was liberated by the Guards Division on 3rd September and 11th Armoured Division reached Antwerp a day later. In Brittany, the German garrisons in the major ports put up a brave struggle to prevent the facilities falling into Allied hands. St Malo fell on 14 August, but Brest did not capitulate until 19 September after much heavy fighting and an effective German demolition of the facilities. The Germans in Lorient and St Nazaire were left bottled up in their fortresses until the end of the

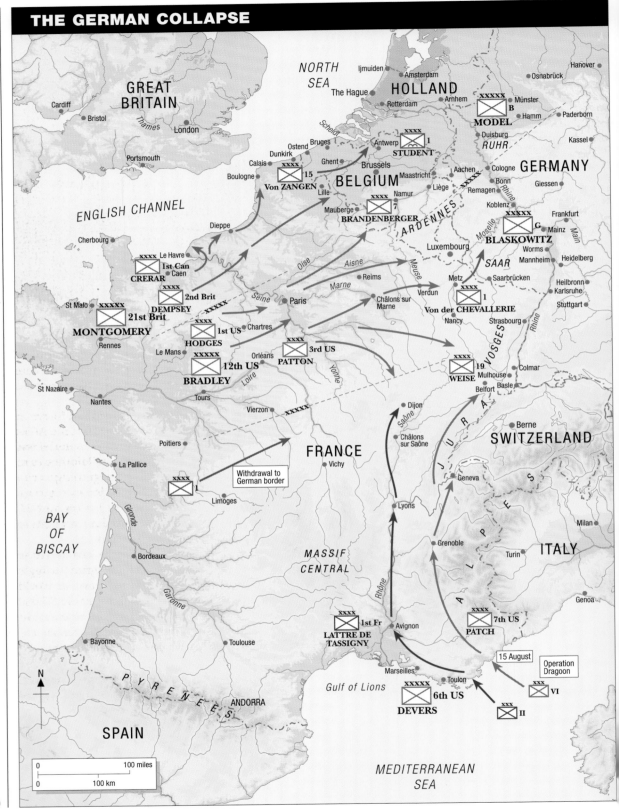

NORTH SEA

GREAT BRITAIN

Cardiff
Bristol
London
Portsmouth

ENGLISH CHANNEL

Cherbourg

St Malo

**MONTGOMERY** XXXXX **21st Brit**

Rennes

Le Mans

St Nazaire

Nantes

BAY OF BISCAY

Bordeaux

Garonne

Bayonne

Toulouse

SPAIN

P Y R E N E E S

ANDORRA

N

Ijmuiden
Amsterdam
The Hague
Rotterdam
HOLLAND
Arnhem

Ostend
Dunkirk
Bruges
Ghent
Calais
Boulogne

XXXX **15** **Von ZANGEN**

Dieppe

Le Havre XXXX **1st Can** **CRERAR**
Caen

XXXX **2nd Brit** **DEMPSEY**

XXXXX

XXXX **1st US** **HODGES**
Chartres

XXXXX **12th US** **BRADLEY**

Loire

Tours

Vierzon

XXXXX

Poitiers

La Pallice

XXXX **1**

Limoges

Withdrawal to German border

FRANCE

Vichy

MASSIF CENTRAL

Rhône

Antwerp XXXX **1** **STUDENT**

Brussels
Maastricht
Namur
Liège
Mauberge

XXXX **7** **BRANDENBERGER**

Lille
BELGIUM

A R D E N N E S

Luxembourg

Seine
Paris

Oise
Aisne
Reims
Marne

Orléans

XXXX **3rd US** **PATTON**

Yonne

Châlons sur Marne

Meuse
Verdun

Metz

XXXX **1** **Von der CHEVALLERIE**

Nancy

Hanover
Osnabrück

Münster XXXXX **B** **MODEL**
Hamm
Paderborn
Duisburg
RUHR
Kassel

Aachen
Cologne
GERMANY
Bonn
Remagen
Giessen

Koblenz

Rhine

Moselle

XXXXX **G** **BLASKOWITZ**
Frankfurt
Mainz
Worms
Mannheim
Heidelberg

SAAR
Saarbrücken

Heilbronn
Karlsruhe
Stuttgart

Strasbourg

XXXX **19** **WEISE**
Mulhouse
Colmar
Belfort
Basle

Dijon

Saône

Châlons sur Saône

J U R A

Geneva

Lyons

SWITZERLAND
Berne

Grenoble

A L P E S

Milan

ITALY

Turin

Genoa

XXXX **1st Fr** **LATTRE DE TASSIGNY**
Avignon

Marseilles

Gulf of Lions

XXXXX **6th US** **DEVERS**

Toulon

XXXX **7th US** **PATCH**

15 August

Operation Dragoon

XXX **VI**

XXX **II**

MEDITERRANEAN SEA

0        100 miles
0        100 km

war; their usefulness to the Allies had been negated by the capture of the Channel ports. The enemy there could do little harm and no one wished to risk losing more American lives for what had become insignificant objectives.

In early September it appeared that the collapse of German forces in the west was complete and that the war might soon be over. But the Allies had outrun their supply lines. Fuel, ammunition and other matériel was still being landed over the Normandy beaches hundreds of kilometres to the rear. The fuel tanks of the rampaging divisions were beginning to run dry. Eisenhower called for a pause in the advance in order to regroup. The delay was fatal. In the brief respite the Germans also regrouped, manned the Siegfried Line defences, and gathered sufficient strength to continue the struggle in the west for another nine months.

The battle of Normandy was as bitter a campaign as any of those fought by the Allied forces during World War II. The grim struggle compared with the horrors witnessed on the Western Front in World War I. The Allies suffered 209,000 casualties, of which almost 37,000 were killed. Added to these were the lives of almost 28,000 aircrew lost during the battle and in the preparatory bombing campaigns associated with *Overlord*. German losses were even heavier. Between 6 June and 29 August the German armies in the West suffered over 200,000 killed and wounded and lost about the same number as prisoners of war. The overwhelming proportion of these losses were suffered in the maelstrom of the Falaise pocket.

# THE BATTLEFIELD TODAY

In common with all the battlefields in Normandy, except the D-Day beaches themselves, there are few tangible remains of the fighting left for the visitor to see. The lanes, fields and rivers that were once choked with bodies have been returned to the care of French farmers, but the bridges, byways and hills, over which the two German armies made their escape, remain and their significance in the drama that unfolded around them can still be imagined.

A good place to begin any visit to the Falaise battlefield is the Polish memorial on the heights of Mont Ormel, close to the Chambois–Vimoutiers road. The nearby museum and visitor centre has a very good display that explains the progress and culmination of the battle. From the terrace outside one is given a magnificent panoramic view over the Dives valley, allowing you to follow the events surrounding the closing of the pocket and the great German withdrawal almost as if tracing the drama on a map.

Colonel Warabiot briefs a group of Free French officers about enemy positions prior to the closing of the gap near Chambois. (Imperial War Museum, B9430)

Down in the valley the medieval keep at Chambois looms over monuments to the fighting that took place in the narrow streets of the town. Just over a kilometre along the road to Trun is a small lane to the left that leads down to the ford at Moissy, one of the crossing places over the Dives used by the escaping Panzers. Leading to the east from Moissy, running parallel to another from St Lambert, is one of the two lanes that led onto the escarpment of Mont Ormel. St Lambert sur Dives is another kilometre along the road towards Trun. The village has been rebuilt since Major Currie won his VC and a tablet in the square describes the fighting that went on amongst its houses. Yet further along the road is the Canadian Battlefields Foundation viewing area, which offers an explanation of the battle to close the pocket. A three-dimensional map, allows the visitor to identify the important sites in the locality.

Beyond the church in St Lambert, near the mill, is the road bridge across which so much of the German transport and armour escaped from the pocket. Through the trees can be seen a narrow foot bridge close to the point where Paul Hausser, the commander of Seventh Army, made his escape. Leading eastwards from St Lambert is the narrow lane up and over Mont Ormel. The lane was once choked with burnt-out vehicles, smashed tanks, dead horses and the bodies of countless men caught by Allied gunfire and the screaming rockets of marauding fighter-bombers. It was along this lane and through the fields on either side that so many of the senior German commanders made their escape. Looking now at the peaceful pastoral scene it can be difficult to comprehend the events that took place here 60 years ago.

In Falaise the great medieval castle, birthplace of William the Conqueror, still dominates the town with its massive keep. Like the rest of Normandy, Falaise has been rebuilt and now plays host to the countless

The price of defeat. A dead SS-Unterscharführer (corporal) of 12th SS Panzer Division 'Hitlerjugend' lies dead in the streets of Falaise. On his left sleeve he wears the 'Adolf Hitler' cuff title of the 1st SS-Panzer Division 'Leibstandarte', indicating this was probably his original parent unit. A cadre of experienced NCOs and officers from the 'Leibstandarte' stiffened the 'Hitlerjugend' Division when it was first formed in 1943. (M.M. Dean/National Archives of Canada, PA-161965)

visitors who come to enjoy its historical attractions. Near the castle is a military museum, the 'Musée Août 1944', dedicated to the battles that took place near the town, with many examples of the tanks and weapons involved in the struggle. North along the road to Caen are the Canadian battlefields of Operations *Totalise* and *Tractable*. Rolling hills, scattered villages and small woods make for a picturesque countryside, but these features were endowed with a more sinister significance in 1944 when each had to be wrested by force from a determined enemy.

Hill 140 now has a monument to the men of the British Columbia and Algonquin Regiments who lost their way and strayed onto the hill to be decimated by the Panther tanks and Panzergrenadiers of 12th SS-Panzer Division. North of Potigny, on the other side of the Caen–Falaise highway, is the other important height of Hill 195, eventually captured by the Argyll and Sutherland Highlanders of Canada. Further north, near Langannerie is the only Polish cemetery in Normandy. In the past, whilst Poland was under communist rule, it was maintained by the French government together with Poles in exile. The railings by the entrance display the crests of the Polish regiments who fought in the Polish 1st Armoured Division.

Four kilometres further north along the main road is the Canadian Military Cemetery at Bretteville sur Laize, although it is actually located just outside of the village of Cintheaux. This is one of two Canadian cemeteries in Normandy; the other is at Beny sur Mer near Courseulles. It was near here that Kurt Meyer watched the Canadian 4th Armoured Division massing for its attack during the second phase of Operation *Totalise*, making the decision to withdraw some of his forces before the US Eighth Air Force's bombing raid. Opposite the cemetery, across the busy four-lane highway, is the ground over which German tank ace Michael Wittmann advanced to his death, towards St Aignan, with his unit of Tiger tanks.

The British breakout battles of Operation *Bluecoat* took place on the other side of the Orne in an area known as the 'Suisse Normande'. The fighting took place amongst small fields, high hedges and steep hills. A drive through this beautiful countryside will give an impression of the enormity of the problems faced by Second Army in advancing through terrain that had a visibility of just a few hundred metres at best, where every hill was an enemy vantage point and every stream or hedgerow was turned into a formidable defence line. Towering above the region is Mont Pinçon, easily located from miles away by the high television mast situated near its summit. A drive along the track on top of the feature will bring you to the monument to 13th/18th Hussars, who managed to get their tanks up onto the hill and swing the battle in favour of the 43rd Wessex Division.

Beneath the hill is the crossroads of La Varinière, the deadliest spot in Normandy, which was bombarded by continual shell fire for days on end under the August sun. Further along the road to the west, just as it swings round a steep part of the tree-clad hill, is the small stream that checked the progress of the 5th Wiltshires. The tiny bridge there is long gone replaced by a culvert running under the road. It was here that LtCol Person stood in full view in the middle of the road, wild rose in his beret, urging his men to rise up and cross the river, only to fall to a sniper's bullet – just one casualty of thousands in the battle to liberate Normandy.

# BIBLIOGRAPHY

Carell, Paul, *Invasion – They're Coming!*, George Harrap (London, 1962)

Blumenson, Martin, *Breakout and Pursuit*, OCMH (Washington, 1961)

D'Este, Carlo, *Decision in Normandy*, Collins (London, 1983)

Ellis, Major L.F., *Victory In The West*, HMSO (London, 1962)

Eisenhower, Dwight D., *Crusade in Europe,* Doubleday (New York, 1948)

Florentin, Eddy, *The Battle of the Falaise Gap*, Elek (London, 1965)

Hastings, Max, *Overlord*, Michael Joseph (London, 1984)

How, Major J.J., *Normandy: The British Breakout*, William Kimber (London, 1981)

Isby, David C. (Editor), *Fighting the Breakout*, Greenhill (London, 2004)

Keegan, John, *Six Armies in Normandy*, Jonathan Cape (London, 1982)

Leleu, Jean-Luc, *Falaise 16/17 Août 1944*, Ysec Editions (Louviers, 2003)

Lucas, James, & Barker, James, *The Killing Ground,* Batsford (London, 1978)

Meyer, Hubert, *The History of the 12th SS Panzer Division 'Hitlerjugend'*, J.J. Fedorowicz (Winnipeg, Canada, 1994)

Montgomery, Field Marshal Sir Bernard, *Normandy to the Baltic*, Hutchinson (London, 1947)

Stacey, Colonel C. P., *The Canadian Army 1939–45*, Ministry of National Defence, (Ottawa, Canada, 1948)

Weigley, Russell F., *Eisenhower's Lieutenants*, Sidgwick and Jackson (London, 1981)

Zaloga, Steven J., *Operation Cobra 1944*, Osprey (Oxford, 2001)

A PzKpfw V Panther under cover in a Normandy orchard. After the first few weeks of the invasion German Panzer divisions were rarely used in any concentration in Normandy, but were committed piecemeal to stiffen local defences or in infantry/tank counterattacks to retake lost ground. The nature of the terrain and the dominance of Allied aircraft made large tank attacks by the enemy impossible; they often became no more than well-armoured mobile pillboxes. (Bundesarchiv, 1011-313-1004-21)

# INDEX

Figures in **bold** refer to illustrations.

Corps (British) 23, 24, 32, 51, 52, 65, 89
Corps (Canadian) 32
SS-Panzer Corps 21, 50, 57
st Armoured Division (Polish) 23, **27,** 51, 52, 53, **63,** 65, **65,** 66, 70, 76, **78–80,** 80, 81, 85, 86
emetery **11**
st Army (Canadian) 9, 14, 23, 24, 27, 59, 60, 69, 70, 76, 88
st Army (French) 27, 88
st Army (German) 27, 88
st Army (US) 14, 23, 24, 26, 30, 32, 44, 59, 61, 70, 88
st SS-Panzer Division 49, 64
I Corps (Canadian) 23, 24, 32, 49, 50, 52, 56, 63, 66, 69
I Parachute Corps (German) 21, 39, 40, 41, 81, 85
I SS-Panzer Corps 21, 40, 45, 48, 69, 70, 73, 77–78, 85, 86
nd Armored Division (French) 60, 67, 71, 77
nd Armored Division (US) 32
nd Armoured Brigade (Canadian) 51, 65
nd Army (British) 9, 23, 24, 26, 27, 32, 40, 59, 63, 69, 88
nd Infantry Division (Canadian) 51, 64, 66
nd SS-Panzer Division 'Das Reich' 49, 64, 70, **78–80,** 80, 81, 86
nd Tactical Air Force (RAF) 22, 27, 51
II Flak Corps, Luftwaffe 20
rd Army (US) 14, 23, 25, 27, 44, 59, 61, 88
rd Infantry Division (Canadian) 51, 65, 66, 70
th Armoured Division (Canadian) 51, 52, **52,** 53, 57, 65, 66, 70, 73, 86
th Armored Division (US) 60, 63, 67
th Panzer Army 20, 21, 60, 69, 70, 71, 87
V Corps (US) 24, 39, 40, 61, 67
th Airborne Division (US) 32, 89
th Army Group (US) 27, 88
th, 8th, 9th Werfer Brigades (German) 21
th Armoured Division (British) 39, 40, 41, 44, 46, 56

7th Army (German) 16, 18, 20, 21, 27, 32, 40, 44, 47, 59, 60, 61, 69, 70, 71, 72, 87
7th Army (US) 27, 88
VII Corps (US) 24, 30, 49, 61, 63
8th Air Force (US) 22, 28, 51
VIII Corps (British) 32, 33, 37, 39, 40, 41, 45, 46, 63
VIII Corps (US) 25, 30, 44, 59
9th Air Force (US) 22, 27, 37
9th SS-Panzer Division 'Hohenstaufen' 41, 46, 48, 49, 60, 70, 81, 85
10th Armoured Cavalry Brigade (Polish) **57**
10th SS-Panzer Division 'Frunsberg' 41, 46
11th Armoured Division (British) 39, 40
12th Army Group (US) 24, 88
12th SS-Panzer Division 'Hitlerjugend' 50, 53, 57, 64, 66
12th SS-Panzer Regiment 58
XII Corps (British) 24, 32, 33, 45, 46, 63
XII Corps (US) 25, 47, 67
15th Army (German) 9
XV Corps (US) 25, 47, 59, 60, 61, 64
19th Army (German) 27, 88
XIX Corps (US) 25, 61, 67
XX Corps (US) 25, 47, 59, 67
21st Army Group (British) 7, 88
21st Panzer Division 39, 40, 49
25th SS-Panzer grenadier Regiment 58
XXV Corps (German) 20, 44
28th Armoured Regiment (British Columbia Regiment) 57, 58 monument **59**
29th Armoured Reconnaissance Regiment (Canadian) 73
30th Infantry Division (US) 49
XXX Corps (British) 24, 32, 33, 37, 39, 40, 41, 44, 45, 46, 63
XLII Panzer Corps 21–22
43rd (Wessex) Infantry Division 39, 41, 42, 43, 46–47
XLVII Panzer Corps 49
49th Division (British) 65
50th Division (British) 39, 40, 41, 46
51st Division (British) 53, 65
53rd Division (British) 64
LXXIV Corps (German) 81
79th Infantry Division (US) 60, 67
80th Division (US) 67
LXXXI Corps (German) 48, 49

LXXXIV Corps (German) 21, 39, 40, 81
85th Infantry Division (German) 57, 58
LXXXVI Corps (German) 21, 50
89th Division (German) 50, 52, 57
90th Infantry Division (US) 60, 66, 71, 76
116th Panzer Division 64
272nd Division (German) 50
276th Infantry Division (German) 37, 39
319th Infantry Division (German) 20
326th Infantry Division (German) 37, 39
352nd Division (German) 60
708th Infantry Division (German) 48, 60

airborne troops 59
Algonquin Regiment (Canadian) 58 monument **59**
Allied air power **9,** 19, 22, 27, 29, 30, 39, 51, 65, 66, 69, 71, **82–84,** 84
Allied forces 22–25, **30**
  casualties 91
  order of battle 24–25
  strategy 26–28
anti-tank guns
  51mm (US) **23**
  75mm (German) **34–36,** 36
  (Bazooka) **47**
Antwerp, fall of 89
Argentan 60, 61, 63, 65, 66, 67, 69
Army Group B (German) 15
artillery
  5.5 inch. gun (British) **6**
  155mm gun (US) **46**
  British **6**
  Mörser 18, 21cm gun **19**
  Sexton 25-pdr self-propelled gun **32,** 51
Aulock, Oberst von **61**

Bayerlein, GenLt Fritz 17
Bittrich, SS-Ogruf Wili 17
Bletchley Park, Buckinghamshire, communications interception centre 28, 29
Bluecoat, Operation 32–36, 37–47, **38**
bocage fighting 22–23, **23,** 27, **29,** 33, **34–36,** 36, 39, **47, 60, 81**
Boisjois fortified manor farm **85,** 86
Bradley, Gen Omar 7, 13, **14, 15,** 24, 27, 30, 32, 49, 60, 61, 63, 88

Brest 68, 89
Brussels, fall of 89
Bucknall, LtGen 41

Caen 7, 23, 26
Caen-Falaise highway 49, 50, **51,** 64,
  **89**
Canadian forces **11, 81**
Chambois 66, 69, 70, 71, 73, 76, 77, 81
Channel Islands 20
Cherbourg 7, 26, 27
Choltitz, GenLt von 81
chronology of events 10–12
Cobra, Operation 8, 9, 27, 30, 32, 44
Collins, MajGen J. Lawton **15,** 61
Cook, MajGen Gilbert 47
Cotentin peninsula **6,** 7, 26
Crerar, LtGen Henry 9, 14, **15,** 23, 32,
  60, 64, 69, 70, 88
Cromwell tanks **70**
Currie, Maj D.V. 73, 76, **87**

D-Day landings 7
decorations
  German **10**
Dempsey, Gen 9, 13, **15,** 26, 27, 32, 41,
  63, 69, 88
Devers, Gen Jacob 27, 88
Dietrich, SS-Ogruf Josef 'Sepp' 17, **17,**
  50, 57
Dives valley theatre 69–86, **71, 81**
Dollman, GenObst Friedrich 18
Dragoon, Operation 88

Eastern Front 20
Eberbach, Gen Heinrich **16,** 17, 20,
  40, 48, 60, 61, 69, 72, 73
Eisenhower, Gen Dwight D. 13, 22, 24,
  26, 59, 60, 88
Epsom, Operation 32
Erskine, MajGen 41

Falaise 73, 91
  German breakout from 71–86, **72,**
  **74–75**
  German encirclement at 59–64, **62,**
  69–71
present day scene 92–93
Foulkes, MajGen Charles 15
Funck, Gen Hans von 49
Fusiliers Mont Royal (Canadian) **73**

German artillery 20–21
German commanders 13, 15–17
German forces 18–22
  casualties 87, **87, 88,** 91, **93**
  decorations **10**
  degradation of 20
  order of battle 21–22
  quality of in Normandy 18–19
  retreat of **90**
  strategy 28–29
Gerow, MajGen 67
Gersdorff, GenMaj Rudolf-Christoph
  von 18, 19, 73, 76, 77

Goodwood, Operation 8, 22, 23, 32
Greyhound M8 armoured car **23**
Guards Armoured Division 40

Haislip, MajGen Wade 47, 60, 63
Harris, ACM Arthur 28
Hausser, SS-Ogruf Paul **16,** 16–17, 20,
  59, 61, 70, 72, 73, 77, 85
Hill 159 65, 66
Hill 195 57, 58
Hill 226 37, 39
Hindle, Brigadier 41
Hitler, Adolf 15, 20, 29, 44, 47–48, 49,
  60, 61, 68, 69
Hodges, LtGen Courtney 14, **15,** 24,
  61, 70, 88
Horrocks, LtGen Brian **14,** 44, 63, **66**
horses **48, 64**

Kitching, MajGen G. 53
Kluge, GFM Hans Günther von 15, **16,**
  20, 27, 29, 32, 39, 40, 44, 47, 48, 59,
  60, 61, 68, 69

Leclerc, Gen Jacques Philipe 60
Lorient 89
Luftwaffe
  III Flak Corps 20
Lüttich, Operation (Mortain counter
  attack) 47–49
Lynn, MajGen L.O. **14**

McBride, MajGen 67
McLain, BrigGen Raymond 71
McNair, LtGen Lesley 30
Maczek, MajGen S. 53, **63,** 70, 76, 85,
  86
medical treatment **77**
Meindl, Gen 81
Meyer, SS-Staf Kurt 53, 56, 85
Middleton, MajGen Troy 44
Model, GFM Walther 69, 73, 77
Montgomery, Gen Sir Bernard 7, 8, 9,
  13, **13, 14, 15,** 24, 27, 32, 41, 49, 59,
  60, 63, **63,** 64, 69, 88
  divisional commanders of **13**
Mortain counter attack (Operation
  Lüttich) 47–49, 59, 61
mortars
  M1 81mm (US) **10**
  Nebelwerfer 15cm **19,** 21

Normandy campaign
  beachhead **6**
  breakout 30–47, **31**
Normandy fortresses 59, 89, 91

Oberkommando der Wehrmacht
  (OKW) 15, 20, 44, 60, 61, 68
Ormel, Mont **78–80,** 80
Overlord, Operation 7

Panther tanks **20, 50,** 56, **94**
Panzer Group Eberbach 60, 67, 68,
  69, 81

Panzer Group West 20, 21–22, 26, 32
Panzer Lehr Division 30
Panzer units 7, 9, 15, 16, 17, 20, 21,
  29, 32
Paris, fall of 89
Patton Jr., LtGen George S. 14, **14,** 23,
  27, 44, 47, 59, 63, 64, 66, 67
photographic interpretation **29**
Pinçon, Mont
  capture of **42–43,** 45, 46, **89**
  road to **41**
Polish cemetery, Langannerie **11**
Polish Divisional Reconnaissance
  Regiment 53
Polish forces 77

RAF Bomber Command 22, 28, 37, 51
RAF Group Control Centre, Normandy
  **24**
Ritchie, LtGen Neil **14,** 63
Riviera landings 68, 88
Roberts, MajGen 'Pip' **33,** 39–40
Rommel, GFM Erwin 15, 28
Ross, MajGen A.K. **14**
Royal Electrical and Mechanical
  Engineers (REME) **24**
Runstedt, GFM Karl von 15, 28

St. Lambert sur Dives **87**
  bridge at **67,** 71, 73, 76, 81
  road from **85**
St. Lô 7, 8, 12, 27
St. Malo 89
St. Nazaire 89
Schmettow, GenLt Graf 20
Schwimmwagen 18
Seine river, advance to 87–89, **90**
Sherman tanks **28, 34–36, 52, 65, 71**
  engine of **24**
Siegfried Line 91
Simmonds, LtGen Guy 49, 50, 53, 58,
  59, 64
Spatz, LtGen Carl 28
Spitfires **8**
strategy
  Allied 26–28
  German 28–29
Straube, Gen 81

Thomas, MajGen 46
Thury Harcourt 63, 64
Tiger tanks **8, 18, 22, 26, 45,** 50, 56
Totalise, Operation 49–59, **54–55, 89**
Tractable, Operation **54–55,** 64–69
Trun 69, 70, 71, 73, 81

'Ultra Secret' code breaking 28, 29,
  49
US troops **11, 12, 25, 48**

Verney, MajGen 44

Walker, MajGen Walton 47
Wittmann, SS-Hstuf Michael 56, 58
Wünsche, SS-Ostubaf Max 58